GHOSTS OF AMERICA
Pikpuk, Inc. All rights reser
or reproduced in any 1
permission except in the
critical articles and reviews.
www.ghostsofamerica.com.

In order to protect the privacy of the people that have submitted stories some names and locations have been left out.

All stories were originally submitted by our audience to ghostsofamerica.com. The stories have been edited by us to better fit this book.

Compiled and edited by: Nina Lautner

Acknowledgements

We would like to thank all those who have submitted their stories to us. These are the people who make our site ghostsofamerica.com and this book possible.

We would also like to thank all the lost souls in these stories. We hope many of them will have found their way by the time this book is published.

1

CONTENTS

1.

Just Beneath The Dirt

Pickens, South Carolina

At the end of Onyx Lane in Easley, South Carolina, there is a graveyard that has long been covered by dirt and gravel. All the tombstones have fallen over the years and are buried just beneath the dirt. Unless you knew it one would never know it was there. I lived in a house at the end of the road for a year before I found out about it. The road was paved leading to the end and then turned to a dirt. It was scattered gravel driveway with a larger circle of ground where cars could actually drive around where the graveyard once was. Like I said it was a year before I found out for myself about the little cemetery.

From day one we would hear noises in our basement that would wake us from sleep, usually a loud thud or crash, and it was always at 4:00 am. When I would investigate the basement nothing was found. Nothing turned over. I found no animals running around and nothing disturbed. This in itself was not too strange until one day I spoke with a lady that lived on the other side of the graveyard. I had not made much contact with my neighbors until I found out the story of the graveyard. This is how I found out about it. A friend of mine had come to visit me one day and brought his son-in-law with him. His son-in-law would not come in the house. He told us a story about how as a young boy he would visit his school pal who lived in my house and spend the night there. He said when he was visiting back then he heard of the graveyard and sure enough after scratching up the dirt found the grave markers and tombstones buried. He said they would hear strange noises at night, usually early in the morning around 3 or 4 am. I had not mentioned what I had heard to my friend or his son-in-law. He said the house gave him the creeps and went to sit in the car while my friend visited.

Once I found out about the hidden graveyard the next day I investigated it myself. I took a rake and after some effort found a tombstone. Even after this my story gets stranger. I saw my neighbor unloading groceries and went out to help her. She was a black lady who lived in the house across from us. She lived with her husband who I hardly saw. He worked the third shift and slept days. Their house was down a hill, and from my house you could not actually see their house. As I was helping her I asked her if she knew we were standing on a graveyard. Her car was parked over it. She looked at me with surprise and said "that explains a lot. " When I asked her what she meant. This is what she told me. She said that some nights she could not sleep and would often get up to get a drink of water. One night around 4 am she said she heard growling and noises coming from her driveway. She went to her front porch and looked up the hill but could not see anything. So she started climbing the steps leading up the hill to the driveway and was shocked at what she saw. Sitting in an almost perfect circle around where I showed her the graveyard was 10 to 12 dogs all staring at the area where the hidden cemetery was. At the time she did not know the graveyard was there. The dogs were growling at some unseen thing. A few were just whimpering. She tried to shoe the dogs away, but they all just ignored her. She returned to her house and did not sleep the rest of the night. She said she was not scared but just had a strange feeling about the dogs. She went on to tell me more.

On one of her late night trips to the kitchen she said she was drinking her water at the kitchen sink. Then she noticed movement in her back yard. After letting her eyes adjust to the night she saw through the kitchen window what she described as a dozen or so men all dressed in long black coats and wearing top hats. She said that was the best she could describe. The strange thing about it was that she was not scared. As she watched, the men started walking around her house headed to the front yard. She went to the front window on the other side of the house and watched the men walk up the hill not using the steps. As they reached the top of the hill, she could tell they were standing at the area where the buried cemetery was. She said under the street light she could plainly see some of the men who had their backs to her. Still she did not feel any fear and decided to go up there to see what they wanted. As she walked out her front door, she could see them up there. However, as she started to climb the steps, they just vanished in a split second. Needless to say now she was scared and quickly went back to her house. She locked the doors and sat there until daybreak.

As strange as all this sounds she was very convincing, but it gets stranger still. When her husband came in the next morning she told him about the sightings. She told him about the dogs and about what she saw that night at 4 am in the morning. She knew she had not dreamed it because she stayed up the rest of the night. Thinking her husband would not believe her she was shocked when he did not act surprised. Instead he told her that he knew about them and that he had seen them too. It was then she found out that her husband could "see things most people cannot. " He told her he had always been able to see spirits, both good ones and bad ones. He told her that usually good spirits will let you see them, but bad ones will hide in the shadows. He told her not to be alarmed if she saw them again. She told me that finding out about the little cemetery made more sense about her sightings. She said she would tell her husband what I told her. We moved out a week later, and I never got to speak to her again. As far as I know the hidden cemetery is still there buried just beneath the dirt.

Submitted by Donnie, Pickens, South Carolina
From Ghosts of America 5

. . . .

2.

My Friend The Spirit

The history of a house has always been a prime suspect in most hauntings: deceased tenants, acts of violence and satanic ritualism, for instance, are fingered in nearly all cases of supernatural occurrences in a locale. But what of a haunting in a home that has no history but what the current tenants know. The home in which I grew up, a two-story affair in the Golden Gate Estates, is a very special part of me. My father had it built when he learned that I had been conceived. The fourth part to his burgeoning family, and the space his current residence provided would not be nearly enough. It was finished less than two months before I was born, and I lived in it until I was eighteen until I decided to move away to college. For that reason, I have always felt a deep connection with the home. Any change my parents ever made to it was met by my unyielding (though ultimately ineffective) disapproval, and it was amongst the hardest things for me to do when it came time to move my belongings. However, many of my childhood toys and effects reside there even to this day acting, to me, like an anchor to which my home and I will be eternally tied. It was therefore with intense surprise that I realized I could no longer sleep well in my own bed.

Six years ago, upon returning for the very first time after my move to Miami, I was greeted with the sensation that I was not alone when the lights went out. In fact, I was certain that each night that I spent in my house thereafter was being closely watched by something or someone at the foot of my bed. Strange odors -- odors that had no business in my room or even in the house itself -- would waft to me as I lay in bed. One incident in particular has stayed with me. On this night, I had, by now, understood the only way to get any sleep in my parents' house was to leave the TV on and silenced. As I began to drift off, something very strange indeed happened. The smell of cigarette smoke, an

8

utterly alien thing in my house for no one at all smoked, quickly permeated my senses. I of course sat up straight confused. I was peering around for the odor's location, but the smell had gone. Perhaps it was simply my overactive imagination having bordered upon dreams. Taking solace in this idea, I laid my head down again, but the smell had returned. I took a tentative sniff of my pillow and realized with a gut-wrenching dawning that my own pillow -- moments ago smelling of being freshly cleaned -- had taken on the stench of a smoker's clothes. I quickly scrambled out of bed and turned the lights on. By the time I had walked back to my bed and smelled the pillowed once more, the smoke odor had disappeared once again, never to happen again. This was an isolated incident, and I may have even chalked up to imagination or even a vivid dream.

Other incidences had occurred around it: a glass of water moving several inches on its own (sans condensation), unexplained creaks in the walls, not to mention the ever-present sensation that someone stood quietly at the foot of my bed. I had always believed in the supernatural, but the fact was that it made no sense for such things to be happening to me. For one thing, neither the house nor the property had any history that would have made it a veritable spot for a haunting: no deaths, no Indian burial grounds, nothing. For another, I was the only one in the house who sensed it. Thirdly, I had not sensed it until after I had left the house. Why now? I have never put much stock in Ouija and, in fact, I have been warned by my mother (who, in fact, has actually seen a ghost before, at a relatives' wedding) not to use such occult devices. My mother has before, and she did not relish the experience.

Two years ago, during a boring day at my fiancé's mother's house, a Ouija board was extracted and set up. I could not resist and I found myself sitting with my fiancé's aunt and cousin, watching my hands guided. Amongst the supposed babbling, prank-ridden responses of an unborn child, the aunt "contacted" another spirit who was much more helpful. Again, I gave in to temptation. I asked about my house, on the off-chance that it might actually know something. According to this spirit, my house and property were the place of a tragic death after all. One that was undocumented because, quite literally, it was never known. Apparently, an escaped slave had perished on the grounds during a hurricane in the 1800s (I cannot remember now the exact year). He was not a prominent spirit by any means and had no reason, I suppose, to appear. The spirit went on to explain that the slave had been a musician and subsequently took a liking to me, as I also had a creative talent in writing. When I left so abruptly, he felt alone again. My returns to the house were very exciting for him, and he would make himself known more often, as if to impress on me his loneliness when I was away.

By this time, however, I no longer slept at my parents' house alone, as I was always accompanied by my fiancé, and so the slave-spirit would not linger. But still, when I went home, I told the air in my room that I knew who he was now and that I understood his reasons for being around. I explained that I was easily startled and that if he could please keep his presence to minimum, to spare me sleepless nights when I was alone. So far, my friend the spirit has thankfully acquiesced, and I have not felt nor smelled him since, though I often think of him when I am there.

Submitted by Bryan, Naples, Florida
From Ghosts of America 3

. . . .

3.

The Young Lady And Her Dog

Ware Shoals, South Carolina

My father grew up in Ware Shoals. He was raised by his mother because his father walked out on the family when he was a small boy. It was his mother and four other siblings that lived with him in the old two story white house. The house was off the road, and neighbors were not within "hollering" distance. The land the house sat on had once been Indian land. It was not unusual to find arrow heads and other artifacts that confirmed this fact. Being a single uneducated mother in depression times was difficult and dangerous, but my grandmother had a shot gun over her mantle, and she knew how to use it. As a matter of fact, I heard that she did use it on numerous occasions to run would-be thieves that had intentions of taking a few of her chickens. There was another house on grandma's property. I heard that she had once lived in it too. It was a two-story log cabin house that was down the path and towards the river.

As a child I remember my cousins and I liked to play in the old abandoned house. In front of the house was a huge tree, and around the tree was an indentation. One day coming back from swimming in the river my daddy stopped and walked over to the tree. He pointed out the unusual indentation around the tree almost looked like the old tree had worn a belt. Daddy began to tell of the pretty young Indian girl that had once lived in the old house as a helper to the owner's wife who was in poor health. The young girl would sometimes walk the path by my grandmother's house on the way to the road to where she would retrieve the mail from the rural mail box.

As there was a shortage of things to entertain yourself with, my grandmother would take her place on the porch in the evening after the dinner dishes had been washed and sterilized. There she would sit in the quiet of early evening and enjoy the cool breeze

11

that was welcomed after the heat of the day had subsided. It was a peaceful place and a good place to be.

However, things were going on just a short distance from grandma's house that would disturb the peace she so enjoyed. You have to remember that this happened back in the country. It was the time before people in that area even had electricity. There certainly were no street lights. The only lights around those parts were given off by kerosene lanterns. The old log cabin down the path from grandma's house was not visible at night. She sat on the porch after watering her plants that surrounded her in coffee cans.

The crickets and frogs along with a few whippoorwills was a type of therapy for this lady doing her best to raise her family alone. The kids were all in bed, and this was "her time". The still of the night would be interrupted by the bark of a small dog. The little dog had been heard many times before and either my grandmother or one of her sons would reach for the shotgun and go out to see what was going on. Sometimes she would point the gun up in the air and fire to scare the dog off. She figured he was trying to get one of her chickens. Tonight the little dog ran up the path and passed right in front of her porch. He seemed as if he was scared, and his barking became louder and louder.

It was different from the barking dog she was used to hearing. She got the feeling something was terribly wrong. The dog ran back toward the old log cabin. Things got quiet again, and grandmother finally got up and went inside. She took her braids down, washed her face, put on her gown, and went to bed. It would have been nice if she had air conditioning, but she did not. The only air that came in was through the open windows. Just before she fell off to sleep she heard the sounds of a lady crying. She sat up in bed, listening and trying to figure out what was going on. The cry became more of a whimper, and grandma got up to peek out the open window. Thank goodness the moon was up and gave a small amount of illumination to the otherwise dark night. In the

12

shadows of the log cabin she saw two figures. It was possible to know what was happening, and eventually things got quiet. It was very quiet, and grandma got back in bed and went to sleep.

The next morning she was up early as usual getting started on her daily chores of which one was getting water from the well at the back of the house. As she rounded the corner of the house she was startled to see the figure of a small woman followed by the same little dog she had seen the night before. Grandmother called out to her and asked what she was doing. The lady turned and looked at my grandma at which time she and the little dog vanished into thin air.

I know this is true because I have heard my father and all of his family tell the story many times. A few months went by, and my daddy and his brothers were going to the river to fish when they saw something strange. As they got closer to the old tree they saw what looked like human bones, a few remnants of a dress, and the skull of a dog. Wrapped around the tree was a chain. No one really knows what happened that night, but my grandmother never forgot it. She could still remember the lady and dog she saw by the well that simply vanished.

What my daddy did remember was that every time they watched the tree grow bigger and bigger through the years, and as the tree grew larger it engulfed the chain as if to swallow it along with the mystery of how it got there. After I grew up I had a yearning to go back to grandma's old place. I had heard the man that bought the property could be difficult, but when I introduced myself he let me go on the property and look around. The beautiful old house looked much the same but had become a storage place and was no longer lived in. As I looked down at the old log house I could not go down there because there were some cows grazing in the fields. I really wanted to see if the old tree was still standing. I may never know, but I do know that on many occasions the young lady and her dog were seen walking in the wee hours of the morning. If you called out to her, she and the dog vanished. My father and his brothers and sister went to their grave declaring that this really happened.

Submitted by Jan, Ware Shoals, South Carolina
From Ghosts of America 3

. . . .

4.

George

Birmingham, Alabama

In the early 1970s my family moved to a two-story-four-bedroom house in Homewood, Alabama. Now the neighborhood was somewhat exclusive and high-dollar. In the 1970s it was much more average with many homes looking somewhat neglected. My brother and I were tired of apartment life and were very thankful to finally have an actual house. Our mother surprised us with news of our new home by parking in front of it and letting us out of the car. On first glance we teased her and said she got a really good deal on the house because it was haunted. We had seen such things in old comic movies on television. We joked. English ivy grew up the front wall to the roof of our demurely green house. The former owner (s) left two old sofas in the living room. My brother claimed them for his downstairs bedroom. I chose a small upstairs bedroom that had excellent natural lighting. Our mother claimed the upstairs master bedroom and declared that our grandmother would have the other downstairs bedroom. We moved in.

Several weeks passed uneventfully. Then one night I stayed up late waiting for my brother to come home from a friend's apartment nearby. I invaded his bedroom downstairs and lay down on one of the two sofas. A few minutes passed. I busied myself by looking out a window at our neighbor's house. Suddenly I heard very pronounced footsteps begin to walk across the floor above the couch. The steps were very deliberate and crossed the width of the room exactly above the couch turning at the outside wall of the house and pacing back toward the inside wall nearest to me. Again the footsteps turned, moved about two feet out, and stopped just above me. Some part of my mind lingered on the odd nature of the steps. I jumped up off the couch and raced out into the hallway and up the twisting stairs. Just as I reached the first landing and turned to face the upstairs portion of the hallway I realized that there were no lights on at all. The upstairs was completely black. There were no sounds at all. I called out my brother's name several times. An unfamiliar feeling came over me. I instantly realized that the footsteps came from the attic above my brother's bedroom. Then I realized the impossibility of anyone walking in our attic.

The attic had no floor, only rafters with a large board in the middle of the floor near the entrance. A person could not walk the width of the attic or even half of the attic because the pitch of the roof created a sharply sloping ceiling. We all had to stoop over to walk in the central axis of the attic. From that point the roof sloped at such an angle that it quickly dropped the ceiling to a few feet in height and then inches. It was physically impossible for someone to walk in our attic to match the footsteps I heard so clearly. I also realized that the footstep sounded distinctly like men's dress shoes with new tight hard leather soles clicking across linoleum. The floor of the attic was made up of rafters. Besides, my brother would not be caught dead in men's dress shoes. He wore converse high-tops. Suddenly I had an overwhelming urge to flee. I was scared to death! I thought everything through again and again. Though it felt like minutes passed it had only been seconds. As I ran down the stairs I woke up my grandmother. I apologized and told her that I thought I heard my brother come home. I rushed into his bedroom, shut the door, and turned on every light. I heard her grumbling through the door that he should not be out past 10 pm on a school night. Our mother was out on a date. I was alone in our house with no one but my old grandmother and something strange upstairs. Eventually, I got into bed with my grandmother and told her I was having trouble sleeping.

That was an understatement! I never told my grandmother or anyone else what actually happened that night. I did not tell anyone for months. I did not know how to understand it, and I did not know how to explain it to someone else. I distinctly felt that I was meant to hear those footsteps and that they were intended for me. I did not understand why or how they could have been audible. I went into my brother's bedroom every chance that I could get at night. I hoped that I could explain away the footsteps. I hoped that the sound had travelled from my neighbor's house. No luck. Months passed, and then one stormy day I shared my odd experience with my brother and our older sister (who did not live at home). My sister was surprised but laughed it off saying that we had a ghost in our creepy old house. My brother casually said "oh! So you've heard the footsteps too. " I could not have been more surprised! My brother had been spending a lot of time in our mother's bedroom upstairs. I realized that he was the only one sleeping upstairs. The rest of our family members slept displaced in various rooms downstairs. I had only spent one night in my own bedroom upstairs when we had first moved in and then managed to fall asleep in our downstairs den nightly. My brother said that he was frequently awakened in the middle of the night by footsteps creaking the hardwood floors into our mother's bedroom and right up to the side of the bed next to him. He said that he felt someone was there watching him but could see no one.

My brother and I felt that this mysterious house guest was definitely male. Our sister looked uncomfortable and said she was glad that she did not live there. She joked and called our ghost George. The name stuck. My brother and I were determined that no one or nothing was going to make us leave. We had wanted a real house of our own for too many years. We were tired of moving frequently and leaving our friends behind. We were ready to accept that we had moved into an occupied space. Although the circumstances were creepy we would just have to manage somehow with our strange new roommate. Through the many years that we lived in the house, our family and visitors experienced bizarre events by the dozens with stories too numerous to mention. George became sort of an unseen family member almost achieving some level of celebrity. Having an experience with him was sort of a rite of passage into our most intimate circle of friends. Our mother joked about George. I had come to terms with his presence though I tried with all of my effort to never be alone in our house with him. I could sense when he was going to become more active. It seemed that the actual hue of the lighting in our house took on an amber-colored tint, and the air became heavier. His energy seemed focused on the stairwell in the center of the house and on the upstairs.

Once I heard our front door shut loudly from the kitchen at the back of the house. Silence. I snuck around each corner and through each doorway until I peeked through to our living room. At the time one of our inherited couches was nestled across the room. I saw a shadowy figure of a man wearing a brimmed hat. He was seated at the far right side of the couch with his right arm on the armrest and one of his legs crossed over the other one. His left arm was at his side. I blinked to make sure nothing was in my eyes. It was a strange sight to behold. His form looked three dimensional. He almost appeared to be made up of shadows that were the size of small twigs all tangled together in the shape of a man. Immediately the twig shapes began to dissipate like tiny wafts of smoke vanishing into nothing. In the matter of a couple of seconds the figure was gone entirely leaving only the late afternoon sun and normal shadows of the room. Although this was weird I did not feel threatened. Somehow I felt more secure during the daylight hours in that house. It was as though his energy competed with the energy of sunlight and could not seem to mount any outstanding efforts for our attention. On the very extremely rare occasions that I might be at home alone for any length of time at night I would stay in our den watching television with sweaty palms. The television tubes emitted frequencies that allowed me to hear subtle changes in my environment. Using my newly discovered personal radar system I could detect even the smallest shift in the room around me. I could locate an insect crawling by hearing the change in room' sounds. I did not feel particularly safe, but I felt that I could sense anyone or anything attempting to approach me.

Being alone there was very stressful to me, and I did everything in my power to keep plenty of activity and visitors in our midst. We typically had a house full of friends and pets. Over time our grandmother sadly passed away. My brother and some of our friends formed a band and moved to Puerto Rico (not sure why that particular location). Our mother remarried and moved to our new stepfather's farm an hour outside of the city. By this time our neighborhood was becoming quite expensive and a sought-after place to live. I was not about to stay in that house alone. No way! By this time I was in college. I moved from our house into a miserable dormitory where I slept on a thin mat and woke to the smell of burning biscuits daily. My college experience was not comfortable. My mother could not understand why I would spend extra money to live in misery when we owned a large home in a great neighborhood. I reminded her that she knew good and well why I did not want to stay in that house by myself. She tolerated my determination to suffer.

Later I left my studies at the college. I married, and we had a son. My husband had been an acquaintance of mine and my brother's since we were teenagers and had loosely heard stories about George. He had never experienced anything though. My brother and his new girlfriend moved back to our family's house from Puerto Rico. My husband and I decided to move there to save money. I felt safer knowing that there would be several of us in the house although I felt apprehensive about having a baby there. I was not sure about how George might behave toward my innocent child. Before we even had a chance to move in my brother had quite an experience. He said that he and his girlfriend had invited a couple of our mutual friends (that were currently dating each other) over to play trivial pursuit. They had been making mixed drinks and having a great time in the living room when all of a sudden there was a very loud bang behind the fireplace. My brother said it sounded like someone slammed a grand piano into the wall behind the fireplace. It scared one of our friends so badly that she raced out of the front door off the porch and slipped on our walkway. She actually left tracks where the force of her fall ground her front teeth against the walkway. My brother showed us her teeth marks.

Now I was very concerned about moving home. Unfortunately my husband and I had no alternative. Though some time passed we eventually reluctantly moved back into the house bringing our baby with us. We used my grandmother's old bedroom as our son's nursery (the room behind the living room fireplace). We moved into my brother's old downstairs bedroom. My brother's girlfriend moved across the country to her original home town Los Angeles. My brother slept upstairs in the master bedroom. So it was now just the four of us living at the house (no pun intended). My brother used my old bedroom upstairs as a work room for doing repairs on guitars. My brother had tinkered with the electricity upstairs and unfortunately had left much of it disconnected. A lot of the electrical outlets and ceiling-mounted lights did not work. We never went upstairs so it really did not affect us.

One night it did make a difference. I had repeatedly found the closet door open in our son's nursery blocking my view of him in his crib. I carefully secured the door and finally grew concerned that George was at play. I did not care for the notion that he would involve my baby in his antics for attention. I closed the closet door again hearing the latching mechanism engage with a click. This time I addressed George angrily but carefully not to wake my son sleeping in his crib. Suddenly a tremendous noise began upstairs above the crib shaking the ceiling above and the walls around us. It was my brother's air compressor charging with air. My brother was at a friend's apartment nearby. I ran into my bedroom to find my pale husband looking confused at the noise. I made him get out of bed and come with me up the stairs to find this incredibly loud machine and turn it off. We headed up. I was not fond of being drawn upstairs in the middle of the night because of strange noises, but I had no choice. The machine was amazingly loud. The upstairs lights did not work. We got to the first landing where the stairs twists and turned to complete our ascent. It felt like years passed as we quickly crept up one step at a time. With my husband holding on to me I leaned into the darkness and pushed the door to my brother's work area open. Instantly everything went to total and utter silence. I turned to look at my husband's face which was so pale it was almost glowing. We raced down the stairs and into the nursery to make sure everything was okay with our son. He was fine. We excused the incident away as a fluke. We all laughed about the ironic timing of everything that had happened that night. My brother reassured us that his compressor would never be a problem again. We forgot about it all and continued with our lives.

Not long after that we requested that my mother babysit and allow us to go to a local nightclub. My brother was working as a sound engineer at this club and some old friends were scheduled to perform with their band. My husband and I had a great night out. As we were leaving the nightclub we looked around for my brother but could not find him anywhere. Some of his coworkers said that he had gone home after our mother called him at the club. My husband and I immediately headed home to make sure all was well. When we arrived my mother rushed past us with her overnight luggage and would not take time to explain her fast departure. My brother came up to us and said "just let her go. I'll tell you about it in a minute. Everything's okay. There's not a problem. Don't worry. " I was worried. My husband had already fetched our baby from his crib and was holding him and waiting for an explanation from my brother. Apparently my mother had a George experience. I was shocked. What could be so bad that she would run out of our house at 3:00 am, drive an hour home, and have to be back in town to work at 6 am?

My brother explained further that she apparently had humored us through the years, but she never believed that our house was truly

21

haunted until this night. She claimed that she began hearing doors shutting at about twilight. She thought our neighbors were having a party and that she was hearing car doors. She said this went on for a while. She finally decided to see how big the party was because there had been quite a few car doors closing. No one was outside. Time passed. Later she thought she heard our back door shutting again and again. She investigated it and found that everything was fine. She said that she checked outside to see if a storm was brewing and found calm weather with no wind. She said that time passed, and later on she heard doors shutting. It sounded like it was coming from upstairs, so she finally went upstairs to see what was happening. She said that everything was normal, and there were no doors or windows open. Everything was secured, latched, locked, and incapable of movement without effort. She could not understand what was causing all of the noise. She said that these episodes of doors closing kept on going, and she would check each time and find nothing amiss. Finally, the doors began slamming aggressively. She began to sense that someone or something was trying very hard to get her attention. She knew that it was not possible for this to be happening and basically freaked out. She had never believed in ghosts. She called my brother and told him to come home right away and bring some big friends. My brother thought there was a human intruder and rushed home immediately with friends as she had requested.

My brother laughed as he told us her story and said "it served her right" since she had not believed us for the past twenty years. It was no wonder that I passed up the opportunity to live in what had become an amazingly valuable piece of real estate for free, so that I could move my family into a costly small apartment in the same neighborhood. I knew that George wanted our attention a little too much. I was ready to part ways with our invisible roommate. Before we moved away from the house I found out from the elderly neighbor next door that the previous owner's son had committed suicide in our home. Apparently he had shot himself and died from the wound. That explained the loud blast that my

22

brother and our friends heard. It explained the male presence we all sensed. It also saddened me to think that the whole time this poor fellow probably never realized that he was dead. To this day I still dream that some invisible force is trying to pull me or lure me upstairs in that old house. It is a distressing dream. I am always happy to wake up away from that house and the persistent and capable voyeur that haunted us.

Submitted by Homey, Birmingham, Alabama
From Ghosts of America 4

. . . .

5.
Bless You

I lived in a house in 2012 on South Boulevard. We were there renting for almost a year. Strange things started happening after a few months. It was a two story house and many of the sounds and footsteps were up the stairs on the landing and on the stairs. We would nightly hear footsteps going up and down the stairs. I would be working upstairs looking out over the side entrance and parking area. Then I would hear someone drive up, get out of their car, walk up the steps toward the door, and no one would ever knock. I would look out, and no one was there. My grand baby, during broad daylight as we enjoyed the front yard on a blanket or in her bouncer, would stare at the front door like she was watching someone on the front porch. If you picked her up and turned her facing the road, she would turn her head toward the front door. She was two months to eight months while we lived there.

The last thing that finally drove us to move out was when I was home alone one night. I could not sleep for some reason. My bed faced the kitchen door with full view of the whole kitchen, where the stairs ended. I always kept the bedroom door open while I slept because it made me feel less closed in. The house seemed more "full" this one night. Air felt heavy. I was sitting in bed reading and heard someone walking above me upstairs, which was very normal. The footsteps came down the stairs, so I instinctively looked up the kitchen, which always had the light on above the sink to light the room. It was less creepy that way. When I looked up I saw a dark mass round the corner out of the stairs, and it came into the kitchen. There was my microwave table against the left wall of the kitchen. This thing seemed to look right at me, and seem to realize I was staring right at it. Then it ducked behind the table. It was about four feet tall and was a human shape. It made no noise. It just crouched there. I could

24

clearly see the top of the head of it. I was in shock and just sat there staring at it. I phoned my boyfriend to see when he was coming home. It was 3:00 am or so, and I knew he was going to be home before 5:00 am. He said he would be home as usual.

During my conversation this thing just crouched there. I did not know what to do. I was shaking and frozen in disbelief. I got up the nerve to shut the door to the kitchen after about ten minutes. Then I just waited and tried not to think about it. I had no way to leave with no car, and I did not want to look stupid by calling the police. So I just waited till my boyfriend got home. He said nothing was there, and he checked the whole house. There were many other experiences, like hearing something crawling in the walls, seeing a face of another person in the mirror of the hall bathroom, and hearing voices having a conversation upstairs. Then you went upstairs, and it sounded like it was downstairs. Small items went missing, and we would find them in plain sight where you had already looked. We made the decision, for my son who was eleven at the time and for the grand baby whom I kept during the day, to move out. I just could not take it anymore.

The house was built in 1930. We have been trying to find out more about the house. Through a friend, we now know that the couple that rented the house after us had some terrifying things happen to them. They cut their year-lease short after having a man's voice in the wife's ear one night that clearly said "bless you" after she sneezed when she was home alone.

Submitted by Cheryl, Silverhill, Alabama
From Ghosts of America 4

. . . .

6

The Strangest Things Of All

Lafayette, Louisiana

The house we used to live in had some very interesting things going on. I never saw anything except out of the corner of my eye, but I always held that suspect. I did not, however, hold the way a room would suddenly get very cold suspect nor did I hold the constant awakening at night by footsteps going up and down the wooden staircase to be so. I would get up when thus awakened and go to each of the different bedrooms to see if anyone was going up and down the stairs. No one was ever sleepwalking, and the older kids had moved out. I thought it was odd, but I did not really want to dwell on all the possibilities. The younger girls both had very strange experiences when they were younger that led me to question neighbors who had been on our street much longer. My older daughter when she was either three or four stopped me one day demanding to know who "the old lady in front of the pinball machine was. " When I told her that I did not see any lady she got frustrated and insisted on pointing toward the pinball machine. The third time she began to insist she turned and looked once again toward the pinball machine. This time, however, she shrugged her shoulders and said "oh, it's okay, mommie. She's gone. " Then she went off to play.

Now the pinball machine was something we had agreed to buy from the former owners. It had belonged to the son. Had I understood the connection at the time I do not think I would have agreed to buy it. A couple of years later her younger sister who is even more sensitive came to me at the age of three when I was washing dishes in the kitchen. She pulled on my pant leg. I looked down at her asking her what she needed. She pointed over toward the formal dining room and said "mom, who's that man?" I looked and of course saw no one. (Seeing someone has not been my gift.) She got a little frustrated and said "mom, that man over there, the one with the gun!" I pretended to be cool and assured her that I

26

did not see anyone. Then like her sister before her she looked back shrugged her shoulders, and in her little lisp said "it's okay. He's gone now. " Now I had heard a few stories from neighbors because I had begun asking questions not long after we moved in. I kept getting goose bumps when the room would go really cold and a horrid feeling that someone was watching me. I remember asking a next door neighbor if something had happened there to which she nodded slowly looking over at our house. "Oh, yes" she said "that boy killed himself. " Now because my husband had kept insisting that I was only the victim of an overly active imagination I felt justified. I did not ask the neighbor where the boy had committed suicide, but I did ask her why. She said that he had asked to borrow a very expensive car that his parents had bought after making money quickly off of some kind of oil deal.

After both girls got older, and each had seen someone first the old lady and then the young man, I was outside with the kids gardening in the front yard while they were riding their bicycles on the driveway. It was getting late, and the sun was almost completely set. There was a grandmother walking her little grandchild in a stroller in front of our house. She kept stopping in front of our house and looking at us. The third time she did this I got up and walked over to her introducing myself and asking her if she knew anything about the house. At that point she looked strangely at the house almost as though she were afraid and said "oh, yes. I knew the people who used to live here. " I said "that boy killed himself here, didn't he?" She said "oh, yes. He took the car and wrecked it and was very afraid of what his parents would say. So he got the gun. That's when he killed himself. " I asked how long ago that had been. It seems to have happened in either the late seventies or very early eighties. A few weeks after that a neighbor from across the street brought up the subject on her own and told me about how the boy had shot himself in the upstairs room where my younger daughter was living at the time. Everything began to fall into place.

In a strange sort of way I felt justified, but I did not know what to do. I tried to ignore it, but after something happened I could not do it anymore. We were having some remodeling done in the house. This seems to have had a negative effect on the energy still there. One day when it was going on I was working on a book in the study. It was the summer and the girls were sitting together just inside the door. My younger daughter was whispering to my older daughter who began to verbalize the problem. She said "mom, do you ever feel as though somebody is in the room looking at you even nobody is there, you know, you get cold, and you get goose bumps?" I did not want to scare my girls more than they were already obviously scared, so I lied and said no. My older daughter looked at her little sister and said "well, Rach says that sometimes she feels like that and sometimes I do too. " At that point I clearly knew I had to do something. I called my cousin who pointed me to a little place close to the public library over on Congress Street. One day I went into the place and was told to wait for a woman who came out of the back of the store. She looked at me and said "oh, you're the woman who's come to see about that boy, aren't you? He's giving you and your girls trouble. " Now I want the reader to know that I had said nothing to anyone at the store. When I questioned my cousin, she said she had not done so either, so my question is still how did she know?

However, she told me what to do. I did them and things quieted down for a few months. After a while things began to act up again especially after the remodeling we had planned was over. The last thing that happened in relation to that house was that one Sunday afternoon the sister of the boy who killed himself came to visit quite unexpectedly. She asked to see all the things we had done to change the house. I remember specifically because I found it odd. On that day I was baking something cinnamon and the scent carried all through the house. She seemed fine. A month later we learned that she too had shot herself even though she had two small children. Her father-in-law was the one who found her just before she died. He asked her why, but all she said was that "I had to," and then she died.

After my husband was killed, then it was something of a relief to move out. Our new house does not have the problems of the old one. As an aside the person who bought the old house began changing the remodeling we had done back to the way it was before we had bought the house. I know the neighbors agreed that what we had done was an improvement. It was very strange to see the house return to its old look. I have also since learned that spirits do not like such changes. I know that many people may find my story strange-to say the least- but I promise that it is all quite real, and perhaps that is the strangest thing of all.

Submitted by Melody, Lafayette, Louisiana
From Ghosts of America 5

. . . .

7

When I Was Pregnant

Batesburg, South Carolina

When I was twenty-one years old my husband and I moved into a hundred-year-old duplex. This house was absolutely beautiful with hardwood floors all throughout. There was a fireplace in the den and in the master bedroom. The only bad thing was the location. The house was right across the street from some railroad tracks and across from a lodge. After moving there, the first two weeks all was fine. I became pregnant shortly thereafter. I must admit though that when I first walked through the foyer I had a strange feeling. Maybe it was the age of the house. I was not too sure. It was just something stirring in my soul. It was very difficult to explain the feeling. One morning I awoke, and my husband was already at work. It was about 7:00 am, and the sun was just rising. Starving, I half-asleep walked to the kitchen and fixed me a bowl of Fruit Loops. I was so hungry. I just dove right into that bowl of cereal. Crunching away and thinking about how yummy these fruity circles were, I was in heaven. I was in mid-crunch, and I heard a woman sneeze in my right ear as if she were standing right behind me. I was confused.

I was not scared. I was just thinking "Hmm. Maybe the neighbor living on the other side of the house was home. " It was a really loud sneeze. I of course set my bowl down and began investigating my robe. I walked outside to the backyard and did not see anyone, so I ran back inside and out the front door as fast as my preggo feet could go. I got to the porch and glanced to the front drive where the neighbor usually parked, and no one was home. Strange! I could have sworn I heard a woman sneeze in my ear. I told my husband later that night about my experience. I really did not think he would believe me, but he would soon have his own experience. We lived there for about eight months before deciding to move somewhere to raise our little baby girl. At the time we also had a roommate. He was a marine. He was a big teddy bear but did not scare easily. My husband, our roommate, my younger sister, and I all had experiences while living in this duplex. One day my younger sister and I were talking in the living room. We had a couple candles going because for some reason the house was always dark. All of a sudden a candle snuffed out, and the smoke coming off the candle went in a straight line completely sideways. It freaked the both of us out, so we decided to go hang out at my sister's house.

One night my husband and I went to bed after our friends had gone home. Around 3:00 am I was startled out of my sleep by something I had never experienced before in my life. I fell asleep nice and snug against my husband. It was around Halloween when the spirits tended to be more active. So what startled me out of my sleep? It was a touch on my left foot. It was icy as I am sure most people would describe it, but it was also an electric sensation. It was tingling hot and cold at the same time. It was like when you touch your tongue to a battery. I reached down to touch it, and it was ice cold to the touch, just that one area on my foot. The rest of my foot was very warm. We also had a heating blanket on the bed, so we would be extra warm because it was always cold in that house. My husband was sure it was a pregnancy thing, and that it was completely normal to have tingly feet.

A few days later and Halloween had passed, and we were returning from dinner. Our roommate was home since we saw his truck in the driveway. We made our way into the house through the living room and into the hallway heading to our bedroom. We glanced in our roommate's room to find him rocking on the side of the bed (with his knees to his chest.) He was dazed just staring into his closet that was wide open. It took our roommate a moment to even realize we were there. Then in a shaky and uneasy voice he said "dude, I...I swear, I have been hearing weird stuff all night. I don't know if I am going crazy, and it's all in my head or what. " I said "what in the world are you talking about?" He replied "I swear to you, I was lying in bed and saw in the far

31

corner a dark blob thing, and it was getting bigger and bigger. Then I heard a baby crying from my closet. " (I am getting chills just recalling this because that place was freaky.) He then said that his cat and our cat were going crazy all night. Then after he heard the baby cry his cat just sat as still as ever (along with him) and stared into the closet. His cat was still staring and sitting right in front of the closet when he was talking to us. Our roommate then got up and stormed into the kitchen. He said that right after the baby cry sound he heard a loud bang from the kitchen. To demonstrate the sound he picked up a large can of fruit cocktail and slammed it onto the floor. "Bam!! like that. " He was quite shaken. Then he asked us to never leave him there alone again. He said if we were going out after work, we should let him know because he was not going to come unless someone else was in the house.

Night after night we would hear things in the early morning hours. There were shadows that grew in our rooms hovering over our beds. I thought I was losing it for a while there. I remember one night. I was so terrified of being touched or seeing that black nothingness growing above me that I sat on my bathroom floor with the lights on all night long. Needless to say I slept the entire day away after that. Then for a while there nothing had happened. December came, and it started up again. One night I was playing the piano working on one of my songs when our roommate stormed into the living room and stopped right beside me. He shouted "did you hear that?" Then he went to the front door and looked out. He turned around with a confused look on his face. He said there was a loud banging at the door. He beat his fist against the door and said "like this. " Surely if it was that loud and at this door, I would have heard it over the piano. So we agreed it was weird, and he went back into our room to play a video game with my husband. Apparently my husband had heard it too but sent our roommate to check it out. I must admit after he was out of the room I heard something odd. I was playing the piano and had stopped a moment to try to "feel" the music, and I heard something hit the floor beside the piano. It sounded like my pencil that I was using to write my lyrics. I glanced down, and there was not a thing on the floor, and my pencil was still on the piano. I assumed it was just the floorboards creaking and continued to play the piano.

Every night we would hear loud heavy footsteps like that of a boot. All throughout the house they would echo. Our roommate wore boots. Most of the time I figured he just could not sleep, and he was restless. Little did I know that it was not our roommate at all. This particular night I heard the footsteps coming down the hall into the living room and out onto the porch just outside our bathroom. Then they came back in through the living room a second time and down the hallway. What could have only been two minutes later I hear his loud truck pull in the driveway. If our roommate was just getting home whose footsteps did I hear just then? I sat up in the bed and listened as our roommate unlocked the front door and walked to his room. I listened to his footsteps to compare, and they were not very loud at all, and yes he was wearing boots.

Christmas was right around the corner, and I was about nearly six months pregnant when the next big thing happened. My husband was lying on the floor in the living room enjoying the music and lights on our Christmas tree. The TV was off, and the glow from the tree was the only light in the room. I was in the very back room digging for my pregnancy book. After about ten minutes of digging through some boxes I found the book and headed to the living room. I casually walked in and sat on the couch. My husband turned around and said "hey, weren't you just in here?" I told him "no, I was in the back room getting this book. " I held it up for him. He said "well, I saw you just walk in and pet Prissy then you walked out. " I thought he was pulling my leg. My husband was a huge skeptic, and to this day he claimed he has not experienced anything first hand. He went on to tell me that he saw a woman in a long dress reflected in the television. The woman was about my height, and I could only guess she appeared preggo. She walked in and petted our roommate's cat, and the cat acknowledged her. Prissy was licking herself, and when the spirit petted her she stopped and looked up at her and like most cats nuzzled against her hand. I went on asking him details. He said she was not very detailed, and he did not stare her down because he figured it was just me.

I had gone out Christmas shopping, and my husband stayed at home playing his video games as usual. When I got back home he told me something weird had happened while I was gone. "Tell me about it!" I was intrigued because Tony is such a skeptic when it comes to the supernatural. Obviously something or some spirit was going to make a believer out of him. He said "well, I was playing my video game, and I thought I heard a knock at the door, so I paused the game. Then I heard a woman say 'hello? Is anybody here? Hello?' It sounded like she was at the front door, so I got up and went to see who it was. I thought it was mom or our neighbor. When I got to the door no one was there, and there was not a car outside either. " I believe it was the woman that sneezed in my ear.

So many footsteps, shadow figures, and some sleepless nights later we were packing to move out of this house. Anyway we were cleaning up the place and loading the trailers when our roommate and my husband took off to explore the woods behind the house. Pretty much everything we owned was out of the house and ready to be hauled to the next house, when my husband and our roommate came darting back out of the woods. They were ghost white. I asked them "what is going on?" They had found two shacks out back like something out of the Blair Witch movie. The only thing was the vegetation surrounding the huts was withered and nothing was growing there. All the plants were black. It frightened them so much they took off running. Right when we were nearly finished our landlord stopped by to get the keys and to give us back our deposit. We just had to ask her whether the

34

house was haunted or not. She asked us why we would ask such a thing, and we explained everything that went on in that house.

Our landlord said that she believed it was. She informed us that at one time she and her husband lived there when they first bought the place, and she was pregnant. She looked down at my tummy and said "yep, you are pregnant. You are the first pregnant tenant that has lived here besides me. " She then said that while they lived there there were many things though not scary that happened in the house similar to what we had experienced. She began her research into the property to look for answers. She also told us that the house used to be opened up. The living room and the kitchen were much larger. About a hundred years prior, the house was the Twin City's Candy Store. In her research she discovered that the woman who owned the candy store died of natural causes out in California. She also told us before it was the candy store the house had once been used as a medical facility where they helped the soldiers that came through when Sherman's troops were burning everything down. Our roommate Travis asked about the shacks out back. She said they used to be the slave's quarters. We were kind of glad to have some answers, and we were all smiling. It was confirmed. We were not crazy. Then the landlord said to us "I wouldn't tell anyone about this because they will thing you are crazy!" Maybe so.

Submitted by Anonymous, Batesburg, South Carolina
From Ghosts of America 5

. . . .

8.

Stay Clear

Edgemoor, South Carolina

I was raised in my great aunt's house which was built in 1908. Two of my three aunts died in the home. The house is on Edgeland Road in Edgemoor. I am forty-seven now, but as a child my parents raised my sister, brother, and myself in this house. From the age of four to sixteen I lived in fear. There was always a feeling of being watched, and I always slept in a small bed beside my parents. One night I awoke and was trying to go back to sleep. I began feeling weight at the end of the bed, and I could feel the mattress press down. It began to move up toward me like someone was crawling into bed with me. We had cats, and I thought one had jumped on the bed, so I raised up to make it get down. When I looked there was nothing there, and the presence was gone. I always got up early, and my mother would have breakfast started every morning before I ever got up.

There was one night I slept in the second bedroom, and when I awoke I heard pans being moved in the kitchen. I got up and walked through the house to the kitchen which was on the other end of the house. I walked into the den which was right before the kitchen door, and the kitchen light was on. I heard the sound of a pan being moved. When I walked through the kitchen door I began to say good morning to my mother, but she was not there. I looked in the mud room next to the kitchen, and she was not there either. I noticed a pan on the stove, but the stove was not on. I got scared and went to find my mother. When I found her she was sound asleep in the bed with my father. I began to scream and like always they told me I must have just imagined everything. That was when I knew it was useless to say anything about what was happening to me.

We moved to a new home when I was in the 11th grade, and it just became a nightmare I wanted to forget. Time makes things seem less important because I later acquired the home after my grandparents had passed away. It was a terrible mistake to move back into the house because as an adult things went from a small haunting to something totally different. As a child I never experienced things being moved or hearing voices of any kind. I had met a girl who later moved in with me. The relationship was great at first like most relationships but soon changed. She acknowledged that she had seen a black form come from the dining room into the den where she was sitting. I knew she believed in astrology, but I did not know until later she was into witchcraft. She had gotten this belief from her mother, and I did not like it at all. It made me angry towards her because I believe in god and I wanted no part of it.

Time went on, and things were bad. When I was in the bathroom one day I noticed a burn which had gone through the tile to the wood on the bathroom floor beside the tub. She had put the bath mat over it hoping I would not notice it. I asked her about it, and she was burning a charcoal in a glass ashtray while quoting some witch spell to rid the house of bad spirits. Evidently something must have scared the hell out of her. I was mad because she almost caught the house on fire, and I knew she had to go. When she left I began to have huge paintings fly off the wall at night. Water would come on by itself in that same bathroom sink. One night I came in late, and some weird deep voice said "welcome home" as I stepped into the front door. I knew I was not hearing things because my dog in the house started going crazy. My dog started acting weird and barking into rooms that no one was in. I could hear the springs moving on my grandfather's bed like it did when I got into it at night, but I was in the other room!

One night I heard a cough right beside me, and I thought someone was in my home. My dog also barked when this happened. I found no one in the house. Lights began cutting on by themselves, and a touch lamp in the den one night went from low medium to high all by itself. My dog began to stay sick, and the vet could find nothing wrong and said it seemed like a nervous disorder of some kind. I finally had enough and just abandoned the house because my luck seemed to be always bad with one problem after another. I knew the house was haunted, but I think my witch girlfriend had brought something in a lot worse. Some people from New York got the house later on, and I warned the wife the house was haunted. She told me she liked the idea of having a ghost. I thought she would eat those words sooner than later. I notice they have not been there too many years, and they now have it up for sale. I wonder why? Everyone should stay clear of this house if you have kids, or I promise that you will regret it. I have lived and stayed in a lot of places in my life and have never had this kind of problem anywhere else. I do not care if you believe, but whoever stays in that house long enough will!

Submitted by Chuck, Edgemoor, South Carolina
From Ghosts of America 6

. . . .

9.
Bad "Ju-Ju"

Selma, Alabama

I live in a house on King Street in Selma, Alabama. The house was built in 1898 and is known as the Stewart-Holmes manor. We have lived in this house for about five years, and since the first night of moving in we have experienced many strange happenings. The first night we moved in we had boxes filling the "grand ballroom. " Around 1:00 am, my husband and I were awoken by the sounds of heavy footsteps walking around the boxes. The sound reminded me of the sound the shoes the nuns would wear in my grade school. We went to look and found nothing. A couple of weeks later my husband and I found that every time we would try and get intimate, our bedroom door would open. After several nights of this, my husband went out and bought a hook-and-eye latch for the inside of our door. That night we once again started to snuggle, and we saw the door try to open. We lay still for a moment, and it stopped. When we resumed our snuggling, the hook and eye latch on the door rose up, and the door flew open! Needless to say, this scared us to death.

About a year after we moved in we went under the house to fix a water pipe. When under the house we found several old bottles and mason jars. We also found several crosses made out of chicken bones (our dog started digging these up in the yard as well) and some old marbles. I thought it would be neat to showcase these marbles in the house, so I cleaned them off and put them on display in my kitchen. After about two days on display the marbles turned up missing. I asked my kids and husband if they had moved them, and they all said no. When we went back under the house, we found the marbles exactly where we had first found them. I again removed them and put them in the house, and again they disappeared after a few days. This went on for about six months until I said enough and left them under the house.

A shadow of a woman in a long dress can be seen moving in my kitchen. As I have a habit of forgetting to close cabinet doors, you can hear cabinets shutting in the middle of the night. My young son has the old servant's bedroom. Since he was a toddler he would tell us that his friend "Bear" would keep him up at night playing with his toys. I never allowed toys in his crib, and on many occasions I would go into his room and find toys (that were in his closet) in his crib with him. I stopped buying battery operated toys for my son or even wind up ones because they would start going off in the middle of the night. We have had balls bouncing by themselves, doors open and close without any windows or AC on, and a bluish orb that likes to dance around. Several people have witnessed these things, and I have a lot of family member that will not come to visit because they have seen "too much".

Personally, my family feels at ease with all of this, but we have never advertised that we have strange things happening here. We try to downplay it all as much as possible.

The people we purchased the house from were a mixed couple. She was from Africa and her father lived with them. He said the house had bad "Ju-Ju. " I believe he was the one that placed the chicken bone crosses around.

Submitted by M, Selma, Alabama
From Ghosts of America 1

. . . .

10.
My Three Occurrences

Enigma, Georgia

I have had three occurrences happen in Enigma, all within the same area. Two of the occurrences happened when I was about ten years old, and the last happened when I was eighteen.

Late one night my brother and I were playing in the street next to our house where we lived at the time. The house was located right beside a field in the middle of Enigma. It was not unusual to find arrow heads, and broken pottery in this field. Anyway, we were playing one night in the road under the street light when my brother decided he was going in to get something to drink. I waited outside in the street just throwing the ball in the air and catching it.

I got this feeling inside that I needed to turn around, and so I did. When I turned around I just froze, but not in fear because I was not even sure what I was looking at. It was clearly a human shape, but it was entirely made of light. You could not see clothes, but you could see that it was a man by the way that he carried himself and his masculine shape. He was standing in the grass on the side of the road with the tips of his toes meeting the pavement. He was just standing there. I stared in amazement as he began to slowly cross the street, step by step, very slowly. When he reached the other side, he stopped just as his toes began to touch the grass, almost as if the grass was his boundary.

He just stood there for a second staring straight ahead. Then all of a sudden his head turned toward me, and he stared for a total of maybe ten seconds. You could not make out facial features, but you could tell that his head turned by the fluctuation of the light. After the ten second time period was over, he turned straight again and began walking into the ditch. As he walked into the ditch, his legs were moving as if he was going down a staircase, step by step, which was crazy. Then he disappeared into the ditch, never to be seen again by me. A couple minutes later, fear set in and I ran into the house and told everyone, of course no one believed it except for my mother. I believe in ghosts, but what was unusual about this occurrence is that whatever or whoever it was actually acknowledged that I was standing there.

The second occurrence happened in the house next door, which my grandpa lived in at that time. My friend and I were in the house by ourselves, watching my grandpa's black and white TV. We were quietly watching TV for a while, when all of a sudden we heard a loud thump from the front right of the house. We looked at each other wondering what that might have been. We just dismissed the sound as the old house creaking. About five minutes later we heard the same sound, but it was moving farther through the house, now it was in the bathroom.

All the rooms in the house were connected in a circular shape, so you could tell that the sound was moving through the house towards us. We were located in the back left of the house. The sound was moving down through the right side of the house, towards us. The sound was clearly the sound of a footstep in the house. The time between each footstep and the space between us and it began to shorten. By this time we were terrified, so we jumped up, cut off the TV and ran as fast as we could back toward the front door. My friend was ahead of me.

As we were running toward the door, we could also hear the footsteps turn around and start running toward the door, as if it was trying to make it to us before we made it out the door. As we made it to the door, my friend jerked the door open and jumped out. I wasted no time in jumping out behind him, but as I cleared the door seal a strong wind blew past me from the inside of the house, and very clearly I could hear a sound I can only describe as demonic behind me. It was almost as if whatever it was had reached its boundary, almost as if it could go no further than the door. Needless to say, we never entered the house again alone, and I have never forgotten the experience.

The last occurrence happened several years later in my life. Late one night a friend and I went out to the field next to the houses where the original occurrences happened years earlier. We were looking at stars that night trying to see meteorites. There is a pond located in the back of this field and an entrance cut through the pine trees that the farmers had used for irrigation. We were in the field for a while, when all of a sudden I noticed a dim light coming from the entrance of the pond.

At first I thought maybe it was a truck or a person coming out of the entrance. The fact that it was dead silent in the area dismissed the assumption of a truck. The light was a constant glowing light, but you could clearly see that it was coming out of the woods. If it was a person carrying a flashlight, there would naturally be movement in the light against the trees. At this time I could not directly see the source, just the light from the source coming through the trees. My friend, who was a completely different person from the previous experience years earlier, also saw the light. We were both investigating ideas of what we may have been looking at. We decided to wait a few minutes to test our nerves of steel.

The light had no fluctuation to it, which dismissed the idea of a truck or a person who may have possibly been in the woods at the time. The light continued to emerge through the woods, until finally we thought it was going to come out. The light had continued to silently and steadily make its way through the woods. Until finally it was about to reveal itself. We decided it was time to book it! My friend cut out running and I was not far behind. The whole time I was running, I continued to watch and see what emerged. Whatever the source of the light was, it never fully revealed itself before we made our escape. It was another truly terrifying experience. The more I thought about it, the color and brightness of the light was consistent with the man made of light I had seen years before. I finally came to the conclusion that the man made of light had decided to make a second appearance. Needless to say I have never returned to try my luck again. But I am tempted and may one day decide to return.

Submitted by Brian, Enigma, Georgia
From Ghosts of America 1

. . . .

11.
Hot Lights

Plantersville, Alabama

On a cold fall night in 1975 I attended a bonfire on a Riverbank in Plantersville. I was there with eight of my friends. Most of us had just graduated from Selma High School. We were near a very small church with a very old cemetery on the right side of the church. We had been there for most of the evening. About 10:00 pm a friend and I decided to head back to Selma. To get back to the main road you had to drive a short distance through brush and trees on a small dirt road. About halfway back to the paved road we noticed a bright light above our car. We were only driving a couple miles an hour. As we continued to drive the light got brighter. We stopped the car, and the light flooded our car. It happened so quickly we froze. The fear was indescribable. We realized what was happening was unexplainable. As we sat there totally paralyzed we were trying to rationalize the situation. We knew there was no answer.

Suddenly, the lights began to swirl violently in the car. What started as one big light became many lights in many sizes. After about a minute we both realized the lights were flowing through our bodies. Our temperatures shot sky high. We began sweating profusely. This continued for another minute or two. We were exhausted and could hardly speak. After the lights had left our bodies they continued to swirl in the car at a much slower rate. We pulled ourselves together and fled wrecking the car on the way back to the main road. The car kept running, so we never even got out to check the damage. We arrived back in Selma. After getting home we realized we never even thought about our friends. When they got back to Selma and we told them of our encounter they at first thought we were crazy. But over the next few weeks they all realized we were truly traumatized and had experienced something that had profoundly changed our lives.

I moved away to Atlanta not long after that. What we went through that night haunted me for many years before I started reading about ghosts. I researched the issue relentlessly. I came to realize I had probably been visited by numerous spirits. I also found out, while rare; numerous people have experienced spirits passing through their bodies as very hot lights. All the years of research pretty much had me convinced I was not crazy. I am now, after more than thirty years later, at peace with myself about my experience. I have wanted to return to Alabama, to Plantersville, but honestly, I was not sure I could handle what I might find. Now that I know there are many other sightings, I may finally return and finally put my demons to rest.

Submitted by Ron, Plantersville, Alabama
From Ghosts of America 2

. . . .

12.
Our 150-Year-Old Clunky House

Vilonia, Arkansas

The house I used to live in as a kid on Highway 64 had originally been built in the path of that country highway 150 years before. It had been demolished and rebuilt down a short lane further into the property to make way for the road. Many elements from the original home were reused in building the new house, such as heavy iron doorknobs and locks, interior doors, salvaged wood flooring, etc. We rented this house and its ninety acres from the Johnson family, who used to live in Vilonia and at one time also owned a grocery store. There were a lot of old pieces of furniture in the house, including an elaborate electric organ, settees, tables, and mirrors. Many things were at least fifty years old. My sister and I were beside ourselves with joy to find a clunky out upright in the house, and were delighted to take piano lessons in town.

We managed about six months of lessons before Mrs. Johnson decided to take the piano without warning. It was hers, after all, but my sister and I took it hard. That was the end of music lessons for us. The school did not offer any kind of music classes, no bands, no piano, not even a recorder, and it was an impossible stretch for my parents to purchase a piano. We tried to play the organ, but it was very complicated and finicky. So, there was no more piano or organ music. We lived in this house from 1971 to 1977, and there was a lot of activity there that we could not explain. My parents did, however, come up with some believable possibilities that kept us girls from jumping out of our skins. It was a funny old house. There were ancient drapes on the windows and no air conditioning, so the house always smelled old and musty, no matter how hard my mom cleaned, and she was immaculate.

The first night we were in the house, my little sister and I were petrified by the sound of whispering voices coming from our bedroom wall. We shared a room, each had a twin bed, but we spent that night jammed together in my bed, until we just passed out from exhaustion. After that, we slept on a pallet in our parent's room, claiming our room was just too hot. It was weeks before we had the courage to sleep through the night in our own room, and then only with our dog on the floor between us. The house made all kinds of noises at all hours of the day and night, winter, summer; it made no difference. The house creaked and groaned. My mom always said it was just the house settling. Well, all those years and that was one active house. It never seemed to want to settle, just complain. Some noises were easy to identify: squirrel in the attic, rats in the walls, something bigger under the house in the crawl space.

We had two Dobermans who were great deterrents to any wildlife trying to move in, evidence of which could occasionally be found in shreds out in the yard. We kept that old organ plugged in, even though it was never played. It was only touched when we dusted and polished furniture, a continual practice with my mom. When it would occasionally howl out a sour note all on its own at some odd hour, we were startled, of course, but just chalked it up to somebody must have left it turned on, or knocked into the knob and due to its age maybe a sticky key made contact from the weight of itself just sitting there. Kids got chastised for messing with the organ, even though we did not, and life went on.

One fall evening, the school was holding its fall festival and homecoming and I had the honor of being elected fall festival queen or princess or something for the sixth grade. My mother had altered an old prom dress of one of my big sisters. The other big sister made up my face and pinned up my hair with little finger curls in front of each ear, very 1972. I felt like a fairy princess; it was wonderful. The festival started a little after dark (it was October, I think). I was so excited. I could not stand waiting on my sisters to hurry up and get ready so we could go. I went outside and was twirling around, dancing in my dress. All

48

excited when I heard footsteps in the gravels of our driveway I stopped and looked but I could not see anything. It was so dark, and the footsteps kept coming. I froze in my tracks, and the gravels kept crunching, getting closer, I broke for the front door and could hear something running up behind me, I stopped on the porch, nothing. Not a thing! My heart was pounding and my hair was a mess. My sister fixed my hair, gave me grief for playing outside, and no one believed my story.

One day my mother and dad traveled to a business meeting, expecting to be home not long after evening. I was fourteen, my sister eleven or twelve, and the hours ticked on and on. It was dark, no word from mom and dad. This was before cell phones, heck we still had a party line, and while we were getting concerned, we never called friends or even our big sister in Little Rock. We knew they would be home soon. As it got darker, we brought one of the dogs in. We thought one inside in case the one outside did not stop whatever bad guy or monster might get us. It was really late; the news had already come on. We made sure everything was locked up, lights blazing in every room of the house, and then we hunkered down in our parent's bedroom with the door locked and the dog in bed with us and waited.

My sister eventually fell asleep, but I could not. The dog suddenly sat bolt upright; her ears held up, and stared at the closet door. It was partially ajar, since none of the doors closed easily in the house, the foundation had moved so much over the years. She did not bark, did not charge the closet door, just stared, transfixed, and so did I. The more I stared the more the door seemed to open a little more, then I would blink, and it seemed to be almost closed and so on for what seemed forever. Then I heard my name, in a whisper. I froze, tears rolled down my cheeks. I heard it again, very quick, very quiet. The dog just stared at the closet, very tense, my sister slept on, and then nothing. All was quiet, no popping, no settling noises, only my sister breathing, and the dog whining a little.

I was so happy when my parents got home. They got delayed in Little Rock, but they had no idea how terrified we were. There was an old floor-length mirror with a drawer set in an elaborate beautiful old cherry frame that belonged to the house and lived in the hallway outside my parent's room. I say "lived" only because the silver was coming off the back, and it always seemed that whenever I walked past it, there was a face peering out, or a figure moving in it. Perfectly OK when I stopped to check, but always something I saw out of the corner of my eye. One night on the way to the bathroom, I distinctly saw an old man staring at me from the mirror when I switched on the bathroom light. He seemed startled, I know I was, then it vanished and I never saw it again. I did not dare to tell my parents about these goings on, that would only result in a talking to about us girls being "spooky" and seeing things.

One summer night, shortly before we were to pack up and move to California, we invited a friend to sleep over. We laughed and talked all night, watched TV until the test pattern came on (remember the old Indian Chief on the test patterns? Way before cable) , and camped out in the living room on the floor in sleeping bags with cokes and bags of potato chips and popcorn. One light was left on, in the kitchen, as we were expected to knock off the chatter and go to sleep at some point, summer vacation or not. One by one, we started to drift off to sleep, when the weirdest thing happened. We all three awoke to a series of dots of light of varying size appeared near the front door, and drifted slowly toward and then on the old organ. The dots of light did not move independently, they moved as one large mass slowly from the door over to the organ. They did not change in size or move up or down. They all stayed together and seemed to form a pattern. It was startling, but also fascinating, to watch this light-form drift slowly over the organ, not above it, over it. Then it would fade out. After awhile, it would reappear, from the front door drifting slowly from right to left stopping over the organ and then

50

disappearing. It made no noise; there was not cold air that I can remember, nothing like that.

It was pitch black outside, maybe 4:00 am, and the drapes were drawn, but we thought that while we did not remember hearing any vehicles traveling down the old highway, we theorized that maybe there was a car or big truck even whose headlights were creating this apparition, by shining through the decrepit old drapes. So, when it happened again, we jumped up and grabbed the drapes and shook them. Nothing changed. We turned off the kitchen lamp, nothing changed. It was weird; we were not afraid of these lights. We just wanted to know what it was. The lights made a pattern that resembled a little old bent over man with a bushy mustache and glasses like a little old shoe cobbler. All three of us saw the very same thing. We thought it looked just like a little old bent man, and experienced the same feelings of just plain curiosity. It appeared several times, and did not respond to us in any way, but we never actually approached it. After a while we would sit on the floor and watch in fascination as it made its journey from the door to the organ. Then it quit, and shortly after that my dad got up, and we excitedly told him all about it. That resulted in a "hmmm" and that was the end of that.

The lights were the only apparition that we ever saw, except for the fleeting figures in the old mirror. We often heard whispering or bits and pieces of unintelligible conversation that sounded like it was far away. We wondered if we were picking up sounds from a distance, but we were really far from any neighbors. We wondered if radio programs could be picked up in the wiring of the house. But that was about as far-fetched as blaming ghosts, and would probably get the same reaction out of people had we brought it up, which none of us would. Things fell from shelves, or off of walls. There were strange smells of perfume, the same flowery old perfume (definitely not mine, I was a Charlie Girl, or Love's Baby Soft) in my bedroom, and there were the noises. We never experienced anything like this after we moved from the house in Vilonia. My sister and I never really felt threatened by anything when we lived there, except for whatever called my name that night, and I have personal theories on that one.

We loved living in Vilonia. We had great friends and wonderful experiences, but that house was something else. I wonder if anyone else has experienced similar things in that house. I had the pleasure of returning to Vilonia in 1994 after my husband and I moved from California to Dallas. Driving through, I did not recognize the house; so much had changed with the barn falling down and some big pile of something in the front yard and the front door in tatters. I had the good luck to run into Mr. Sellers. My wonderful principal from Vilonia High took the time to drive us to my old home. I got to meet one of the folks living there at that time, and never mentioned anything about "hey, did you ever hear voices here? " It did not seem appropriate, but it was cool to see the house again. Never experienced any weirdness at the school that could not be explained by a hundred wild kids, but that house was definitely an experience I will never forget.

Submitted by Kris, Vilonia, Arkansas
From Ghosts of America 2

. . . .

13.
The Car

During the early 1980s my brothers and sisters and I attended college in Mobile, Alabama. Since our home was in Jacksonville, Florida we frequently traveled along I-10 every time we had a school break. Along this stretch of interstate, there still remains miles of very lonely highway with no exits or signs of life. But in the 1980s, some areas were just desolate. One night on our way back to Mobile, we were driving near Pensacola and were low on gas. We took the next exit which was the Old Cantonment Road. The moment we turned onto this road we were creeped out because everything was so dark and desolate, and there was no traffic on this road.

We had not traveled far before we started to feel a sense of relief as we saw a car ahead of us. But there was something odd about the car. Even as it continued to drive ahead of us something just seemed a little askew. We could tell that the driver had no working taillights, but we did see some light coming from the car. It was not until we gained on it that we realized why. The car was driving along the shoulder of the road, and the car had a bluish white light all around it. We slowed a bit, and then the car made an abrupt u-turn in front of us. Our headlights illuminating a completely bashed in car on the driver' side, from the front fender panel to the rear. Then we saw the driver, and I know I screamed at this point, because the driver had the same eerie bluish white glow about him. His face was terrifying. Turning around in the seat I watched this phantom car with its phantom driver drive away from us and then just be swallowed up in the darkness. As many times as I have driven past this exit in the intervening years since this incident, I have never driven down this road again.

Submitted by Marie, Cantonment, Florida
From Ghosts of America 2

14.

That Little Room

Several years ago after I had just given birth to our first child my boyfriend and I rented a house in Riverside. All the houses in this neighborhood are old mill houses. They are almost one hundred years old, and the old mill still stands even though it has not been in production for decades. The house we rented had two bedrooms, one medium size and one very small and had a large den added on. We had a rocky relationship back then, and we did not know if we were going to stay together. The house was mostly going to be my boyfriend's; I was still living with my mom half the time and staying with him half the time.

My boyfriend and I both had the large room, and we put the baby's crib in our room. One night I was sitting on the bed with the baby on my lap bouncing him. I had a very strange, almost sickeningly uncomfortable feeling. It sounds so cliché, but I felt like I was being watched. I knew nothing or no one was in the room but us. However, I still could not bring myself to look up. I just kept looking down and would flick my eyes out to the rest of the room and just felt like I should not, so I would quickly look back down. I am not a timid person, but I felt unnerved that night. I just figured I was being silly; I did not think I had any logical reason to feel that way, but I could not help what I felt. I did quickly put that incident out of my mind and did not say anything to anyone.

After a couple of days my sister came to see the house. As she was walking through the house I noticed that she would stop in the door frame of the little room. She would not go through it and out the other door, but she would just stop there and then turn. Something about seeing her do that made me realize that we had furnished and decorated the whole house except for that little room. Everyone seemed to avoid that little room. Absolutely

54

nothing was in the little room, not even storage. We never talked about it, but no one just seemed to go in there. One night as we were watching a movie in the den, which has two entrances, one being connected to the little room. I kept having that strange feeling of being watched again. It felt like it was coming from the little room. The door leading to the little room was more like an outside door than an inside door. It had glass panes in it and I felt a mixture of anger and sadness emanating from the little room that night. I have never felt anything like that before. I literally felt emotions streaming out as if they were streams of sun light. They were not my emotions, someone else's. I felt terror and nothing else. I kept glancing at the door because it felt like at any moment I was going to see an angry face looking at us through the glass panes. At this point I started asking my boyfriend if he had weird feelings about the little room or anywhere else in the house. He is a very skeptical person, and even he said that he did not like the little room that much.

After a while of living there we met the neighbors. They were an older couple and had lived there for a long time. The wife asked us if we knew about what had happened in the house, and I just knew she was going to say something bad had happened. She said that an elderly woman used to live alone in the house. Later her adult son moved in with her after his marriage had failed. She stayed in the big room, and he stayed in the little room. The son was depressive and ended up committing suicide one day while his mother was at church. She said that he did not want to divorce his wife, but his wife wanted to move on. A couple of years after his suicide, the mother died of natural causes. Her body lay in between the living room and the big bedroom for several days before she was found.

After the neighbors told us this I was thoroughly freaked out. They had no way of knowing our experiences in the house; this was our first time meeting them. I told my sister what I had learned about the house, and we had never talked about it before.

Then she told me why she did not go into the little room that day she was exploring our new house. She said she did not go in there because it just felt occupied, like it was someone's room. You know that sense of 'someone else' you get by going into someone else's room for the first time. And I agreed with her; it did feel like that. The air in the little room felt heavy and thick. We ended up not staying in the house for long. He started drinking heavily while he was in that house, and I wonder if it had anything to do with that presence.

I still live in Rome, and every once in a while I would drive past that house and see new people have moved in. There would be toys scattered in the yard, and you just know they have put their kids in that little room we would not even put storage in. I wonder if they ever feel like I did in that house.

Submitted by Ebl, Rome, Georgia
From Ghosts of America 2

. . . .

15.
Was It A Test?

About twenty-one years ago I was single and living in Birmingham, Alabama. While I was working on my MBA at a university I had an experience that I never forgot. I have wondered about it to this very day what it meant. At that time video dating had just come out (before the internet), so it seemed like a good way to meet like-minded single girls. The way it worked for you was this. You paid a fee of about $250 and got the opportunity to have five matches. I went to the office which was in Vestavia Hills and viewed several videos of several ladies. I found a lady that I thought I liked which I will say her name was Tammy (not her real name). The service got in touch with her. The next thing I knew they were calling me with her contact info. I called her up, and we talked on the phone. We seemed to hit it off. After about a twenty-minute conversation I asked her out for a dinner date and dancing at a night spot in the south side. She lived in some neighborhood in Pelham, and I went there and picked her up.

Tammy lived in a nice three-bedroom home in a middle class neighborhood with her parents. She was about twenty-eight, and I was twenty-seven at the time. I met her mother who seemed very nice, and after some pleasantries we left her house for the restaurant. She seemed to be an attractive girl and very nice. The date seemed to go fine. We got to know each other over dinner and had a fun time at the club dancing. I was not one of these guys that were into one night stands, and I generally liked to date a girl a few times before intimacy. The date had gone well, and we agreed to see each other again. We began the fifty-minute drive back to her home. Once I was south of Hoover she directed me to some back roads that she said was a short cut. The roads were dark with lots of curves and virtually deserted. We hardly passed another car. I had the radio on, and we were both just chilling out not saying much on the drive back to her home. After about ten minutes on these back roads I had the distinct feeling that she was staring at me. As I was driving I turned and looked to my right. It was liked she had changed. Her soft and gentle persona had changed. Now her head was slowly turning and tilting from side to side and she had a weird smile on her face, more like an unnatural gaze. It gave me the creeps.

I pretended that I was unnerved and did not notice how weird she was acting. I asked her what was so funny, and she replied in a creepy voice that nothing was wrong. She continued to roll her head from side to side. This was not to any beat of the music; it was in a constant motion with her cheek to her shoulder rolling up toward the roof of the car and then dropping her right cheek to her other shoulder. All the time she continued with what looked like an evil smirk. Her eyes seemed to stare off into space like she was looking right through me. I was getting creeped out, but what could I do other than drive on. Finally her street came into view, and I knew we were at her home at last. As we got to her home she asked me if I wanted to come in for a night cap. I really did not want to. I was creeped out by the experience I had just had with her in my car, but she persisted. She suggested that she would make me a cup of coffee for the long drive back. I was getting tired and reluctantly agreed. As we were walking up her drive way there was a mist or fog in the air and a full moon. She commented on the full moon, and I said "oh yes, very romantic" (I said the opposite of what I felt. It actually seemed spooky). Then she said it seemed almost evil to her, like the night her grandmother died. She pointed to the second bedroom window and said that was where her grandmother died three years ago. I was stunned. Then she volunteered that her grandmother was into the occult. She was a practicing witch and practiced black magic. Now I was creeping out. I could hardly believe what she was saying except for the fact about how she was acting.

We went inside, and the house was dimly lit -- only a small lamp in the kitchen. She left me sitting on the couch and went into the kitchen to make the coffee. I sat there on the couch with barely a light to see. After fifteen to twenty minutes or so she did not return. I got nervous and got up and went to the kitchen; she was not there. The door to the guest bathroom was open and she was not there. The hallway to the bedrooms was dark. I did not want to wake her mother, so I called out in a loud whisper her name "Tammy. " There was no response. I did not dare proceed down the hall for numerous reasons. I went back to the kitchen, but there was no sign of any coffee being made. I went back to the entrance of the dark hall and called her name again in a loud whisper -- three more times; again with no response. I lifted weights and was physically active. I could handle myself quite well, but this was something beyond my experiences. Every inch of my body was saying for me to get out of there.

All together I was in her house probably thirty minutes and did not know where she went. Maybe she crawled into bed and forgot I was there, but I did not feel I could just venture down the hall into the bedrooms to see. What if I went into her mother's room by mistake! Or maybe she was practicing the occult. I did not know, but I was not sure I wanted to know. Could I call the police? What would I say? What was the crime? A disappearance in ones' home? She might be down the hall in a bedroom fast asleep. Everything I had experienced was weird, eerie, spooky, and strange, but there was no crime. No, I decided to make my leave, and I went out the door I had come in through the garage. From the outside all the windows appeared dark. There were no cars at the house just as I had come over earlier that night and had gone in for the coffee and was leaving now. Yes, it still seemed scary outside, and the neighborhood was deserted. I got out of there quick and drove home. It was about 3:30 am when I got home.

Usually I called the girl a few days later to say I had a good time, but this time I waited until Friday to call. When I did a recording came on to say that it was not a working number. I thought that was strange, and I checked the number again from what I had written down from the service. The number was correct, but I got the same recording. It was a nonworking number. After a couple of weeks, curiosity got the best of me. When the weekend came again I decided Saturday afternoon to drive out to her home. When I got to her home I rang the door bell, and a different woman came to the door. I asked for Tammy, and the lady said no Tammy lived there. This time I used her mother's name and asked for her. The lady exclaimed that she did not know either of them. She proceeded to say that her husband and children had lived in the home for three years. She did not know about whom I was asking. I asked her if she had always been there during the last three years. She said yes other than their yearly vacations. She and her husband had just returned from their vacation two weeks ago. She looked as shocked as I did when I told her I had met a girl at this house two weeks ago and had a date with her. She was shocked and I was shocked. She suggested maybe I had her house confused. I thanked her and left. Still not convinced I went back to the service to check her video and contact information again.

Oddly the contact information was the same as what was given to me. The manager (owner) who ran the service who met all the girls and guys that joined the service remembered giving me the phone number. However, he could not place the girl's face. Oddly the video was blurred, and the voice on it distorted. It was like the video was partly recorded over. The face could not be made out, and the voice was garbled. He said the videos were kept in an air-conditioned storage and were not exposed to heat or the sun. He could not explain it; we were both stumped. Who was this mystery girl whose video I viewed, called on the phone and had a date with. What happened that night, and why did she disappear? What was the meaning to it? Was it some test I was to pass or fail? Was "passing" to leave the house? That is what I have come to believe. I am a spiritual person. I think I was being tested by "evil". Had I stayed that night or gone down that hall; maybe I would not have passed. I do not know, but I have always wondered.

Submitted by Charlie, Birmingham, Alabama
From Ghosts of America 3

. . . .

16.

An Old Hospital

I was working in an old hospital in rural Alabama installing a fire alarm system. The place was being remodeled as office space as a new hospital was in use now. Most of the facility was finished already except for the old maternity ward. The place had new paint on the walls, new floors and ceilings. When walking through a pair of swinging doors you would reach a space that was clearly an abandoned hospital. We could see the curtains dividing the beds hanging by threads old and dirty. The HVAC window units and beds had been removed as had any electronics that could be salvaged. The floor was dirty with strange brown stains here and there. None of the lights worked, nor did the ventilation system. It was always cold in there. The place was shaped like an "H" entered at the top. At the fork was a nurse' station with the files of the patients that stayed there long ago scattered about the room. The intercom hung by its wiring. There was an elevator there that descended to the morgue below. Straight down the hall were the delivery rooms. At the end of the hall was a door leading outside where there was a ramp leading down again to the morgue. There were more hospital rooms to the left. In one there were cartoon paintings on the wall. In the center of the room was a baby doll but someone had smashed its head, and pieces of it littered the room.

As we were about to leave I said to my helper "damn! I would not be surprised to see a man in a gown standing around the next corner. " Then we heard someone clearing their throat "ahem!" We heard the shuffle of a foot like someone trying to get our attention from back at the nurse' station. We turned, but there was no one there! I said to my helper "did you hear that?" He said "yep! " We were suddenly finished for the day! The next day one of the workers called me on the radio stammering. He said he was standing on a ladder installing a smoke detector, and a woman ran her hand under his pants leg. He turned to find he was alone. We asked him how he knew it was a woman, and he could not say. He refused to go back in there to finish. Later I found out the reason a new hospital had been built. The number of infant mortalities was staggering at this place. That story was true, every word of it.

The day after the old man ran us out I sent my helper back in there to finish by himself. He was not happy about it, but he went in. Then I heard "hey, Loyd! Check this out!" I walked down the hall and in a patient's room on the right there was a bright sunbeam coming through the window. In the sparkles of dust illuminated by the beam you could see a roughly human shaped blob about the size of a four year old child just standing there! We both stood and watched for a minute, and then I told him to just put it out of his mind and go back to work. It was later that day when the other worker had the encounter on the ladder. He was a navy veteran, about forty-eight years old at the time. They never could rent that office space out.

Submitted by Lucky Loyd, Oneonta, Alabama
From Ghosts of America 3

. . . .

17.

How Would You Like It?

A couple of years ago I was traveling through Georgia and decided to stop in Hephzibah to do some genealogy. My husband and I were driving down a country road looking for an old family cemetery in the area when we saw a young woman walking down the road in an old fashioned dress and asked her for directions. The woman said that she had lived there for only a short time. She had only lived there for forty years. My husband and I just looked at each other confused from her response. She said that she knew another woman that might know of this cemetery because she had lived there for sixty-six years. She directed us where to find her.

As we pulled up to the house the woman and her husband came to meet us. I think they were Mennonites. They spoke of the "living family" who owned the family cemetery and said that the family clan had always stayed together. She asked me why I was not "with the family. " I told her that my family had moved away in 1889 and that we lost touch with that side of the family. When I mentioned that date the husband seemed to realize why my family left (because my side had joined the Latter-Day Saints Church and were being persecuted by the others who did not). He said that everyone in town had a book chronicling the history of Hephzibah, and he ran in to get it. The woman went on to say that this family controlled the town since the 1700s and had intermarried with three main families since that time. She told me where to find them at the city hall and said that I needed to ask permission before going into this graveyard. Then she added "but let me say a word of advice to you. Get out of this place and do not ever come back! But if you insist, make sure you have permission. "

My husband and I went and got "permission" and directions from a woman. When I met her daughter I was amazed how much she

64

reminded me of my grandfather's sisters. But how could that be when there were about ten generations between us? (From the present back to the 1880s when they left). We went to the cemetery; it was up an incline and lined with a rock wall followed by an Iron Gate. My husband stayed in the car to read his book, and I climbed up to it and opened the creaky gate. It was unkempt and looked like it had been vandalized over a period of time. The gravestones were cracked and broken, and trees were growing up through the capstones. As I entered I knew immediately that I was not welcome there. It was as though I heard them say "who are you? What do you want? Get out!" So I spoke out loud that I was there to help not hurt and that I meant no harm. I started to reconstruct some of the headstones to read them and then take pictures. I was reading the capstone of a woman by the same name as the cousin that I had met earlier. It said that she was born Methodist and was going to die Methodist. As I was looking down at one capstone I felt something grab a hold of my foot, and then I slipped. I found myself lying on top of the capstone, but my shoulder was pinned back, so I could not get up. As I lay there panicking thinking that it might collapse under my weight, and I might fall through I heard a woman speak out-loud to me. She said "how would you like it if you were the one who was dead?" I heard the horn of our 93 Plymouth start honking. I struggled to get up. Finally I did and I ran towards the creaky gate and down the hill. My husband was trying to figure out what was wrong with the horn. It had never done that before or after. I jumped in the car and said "get out of here!" We took off and left the state.

A couple days later at the hotel I woke up having a grand-mal seizure. When the medics came they asked me questions about where I was, what my name was, and how old I was. I answered. They had discovered that I had lost the last twenty years of my memory (except for the experience in the graveyard). I did not know my husband or that we had kids together. I had a couple more seizures and then was put on medications for it. I was walking around in a mental fog for about a year after that. I still have not retrieved all my memories of my children growing up. After getting out of the hospital we returned home. My daughter started dreaming about a woman who had followed me home. She was coming around knocking on my bathroom window trying to get me to let her in. She disguised her voice to be someone that my daughter knew and trusted so that she would allow her to get close to me. The reason that I had looked up that graveyard was because I had been looking for one of my ancestors whom I believed had been buried alive. I came to this conclusion because of a couple recurring dreams of my great-great-grandmother, one of which was screaming at another woman saying that woman killed her baby. The only thing was the baby did not die. She did in child-birth. She did not know that she was the one who was dead!

The other dream was of me and my great-great-grandmother as a young girl in a hole. We saw a shovel of dirt being thrown on top of us and smothering us. Apparently I found the woman in the cemetery who knew something about that. Hence her statement "how would you like it if you were the one who was dead?" I still have not found the grave of my great-great-grandmother. From time to time I see others on the internet who are also trying to find her too. What should my advice be to them?

Submitted by Janet, Hephzibah, Georgia
From Ghosts of America 3

. . . .

18.

Encounters At B&B

Monticello, Florida

I have recently closed my own business and sought out work with some folks who own a B&B in Monticello, Florida. I had met them when I had a booth at the "Flea Across Florida. " The owners of the Bed and Breakfast were quite warm and interesting, and so I called and asked if they needed help with their B&B. However, little did I know the B&B was haunted.

When I arrived I learned of their ghost tours but was skeptical and took it with a grain of salt, despite hearing a vast array of stories. I soon had my own encounters and experiences. My first encounter occurred one evening while working downstairs (the first floor). I had gone into the kitchen and being new to the facility had some questions. I entered into the adjoining dining room and saw who I thought was the co-owner of the B&B. Her back was turned from me, and she was facing the fireplace. I was talking to her, but she did not turn or reply. There was a different feeling in the room almost electric like. I turned and looked behind me to see the co-owner sitting at her computer in the library room and looking at me in wonderment as to who I was talking to. When I looked back at the fireplace the figure of the woman was gone.

Later that week I was outside, and I saw again something that I thought was the co-owner walking around the side of the house. I walked over to talk to her, but as I approached she picked up pace and started to head to the front wrap around porch. I picked up pace too, but she was on the porch now and around the bend. I had called out her name but figured she did not hear me. It would not be uncommon for her to be dashing for the phone or to meet a deadline crunch for a specific task. However, when I got to the front door it was locked. I wondered why she would lock the door on me. I walked around the house to the back door and entered to find that the co-owner had never left the house and had been on the computer then entire time.

A series of events have occurred like this including lights going on and off, my phone battery dying within a short time of arrival, strange sounds, smells, etc. One night I was working outdoors after dark, and my dog sat up and started tilting her head to the side as though she saw something, but there was nothing there. Suddenly she whimpered and fell to the ground in a submissive position. I decided it was time to leave.

Another day I was doing some cleaning in the hallway upstairs and was by the original now inoperable enclosed elevator, and I smelled what seemed like pipe tobacco. I thought to myself it must be something that the co-owner's husband smokes. However, I never saw him smoke before. On several occasions I smelled the same aroma in the same place. I recently learned that there was an old woman who used to smoke in that very same spot so that the baby in the house would not breathe in the smoke. Recently I was taken on to do some very time intensive projects and invited to stay for duration of the project so that I could save time and gas money. I have been provided the Victorian Guest Room and for two weeks every night I have been awaken by something precisely at 2:11 am.

I could go on with a variety of stories of my encounters but there are far too many to list.

Submitted by Salli, Monticello, Florida
From Ghosts of America 4

. . . .

19

May 7th, 2010

Vicksburg, Mississippi

I am a Civil War reenactor. I was doing a Monument dedication one weekend for the new Kentucky Monument that was being put up at the National Battlefield Park. We were camping on site, so I decided to go for a walk with my lieutenant and a friend in the same group of reenactors. We were walking up on the Texas Monument and stopped dead in our tracks at the sight of a white blur in-between the two hills directly to the left of the Monument. At first I thought it was a just a small statue of one of the generals or colonels or something and thought nothing of it. Until I realized that it was almost pitch black because it was nighttime, and a statue should not be that bright at this time. We watched it for a second and saw arms rise up and then we saw a smaller blur moving behind the original white blur. It moved slightly to the left then slightly to the right. By this time we were kind of freaked out and started walking back to camp.

I turned and looked at it again as we were leaving and pointed at it. I saw it move way to the right and start moving towards where we were at the bottom of the hill. We walked quickly back to camp. We saw the white blur again right before we walked into camp about a hundred feet behind us. Later when we were talking to an artilleryman about what we saw, we described how something popped out like arms from the blur. Before we could finish our sentence he said "oh, that's Sara! She was a field nurse that was killed over yonder." He pointed in the direction of the Texas Monument. We never told him exactly where we saw the object, so there was no way he could have known to point there if he was lying to us. He also seemed to know exactly what we were talking about.

My lieutenant and friend have since been quiet and tried to think that it was not a ghost or spirit or anything. However, we knew what we saw, and we just did not want to admit it. Later that night I walked to the top of the hill fortification overlooking the crater. When I reached the top of the hill I heard cavalry horses behind me trotting. This was weird because there were not any cavalry reenactors present at this event with us. Draw your own conclusions. Believe what you want of this, but this is my description of that May 7th night in 2010.

Submitted by Matthew, Vicksburg, Mississippi
From Ghosts of America 3

. . . .

20.

The Rental

Mountain Home, Arkansas

I lived in a house on Jordan Road near Norfork a few years back. I have never experienced the things like I experienced there anywhere else. I used to not believe in the spirits, or I should say did not know they existed because I never had such things happen to me like they did in this house. We were renting, and it was an old house built in the 1930s. It had old sheds in the back that had many old things, pictures, and antiques. Everything looked to be the same way they were left back then. They had another shed out there that had a broom maker in it where they made their own brooms back in the old days.

It was a two-story house. I heard the stairs creaking very often, which I thought was no big deal because it was an old house. But then it literally sounded like someone was walking up and down them, and nobody was there. I heard noises a lot throughout the year that I lived there. I just thought maybe it was me, and you know the house was old. My son was then about a year old, and it was his birthday. He was in his highchair, and all of the sudden after everyone was singing him Happy Birthday, he just looked away and was following something or someone with his eyes. His stare was something I have never seen before. I asked him what he was looking at. He was like in a daze for a second, and then he just came back like nothing happened.

After that day he started looking away a lot and talking to it. I tried to ask him what he was seeing and saying. Of course just turning one year old I could not get much out of him. Then one night (my son slept with me) I got up in the middle of the night to go to bathroom, as I was crawling out of the bed it felt like my son was crawling behind me following me. I reached back with my hand and told him to get back to bed. He was. He was actually sleeping soundly. I got up and looked behind me, and this black

71

figure was following me. I ran to the bathroom and turned the light on scared to death! I ran back to the bedroom, and all the sudden it got freezing cold in the hallway. My hair on my arms stood straight up. I got in bed and pulled the cover over me, then a flash of light went off, and it sounded like someone had taken a picture. OK well after that night we decided to move.

My husband did not believe in all of this. At first he thought I was over reacting, but later he experienced some things of his own. As the years went by every time we have driven by that house there have been people moving in and out of that house. I have talked to some people that lived there after me. They have experienced the same stuff. They have remodeled it now inside and out. I have always wondered if that has stirred up the ghost.

Submitted by Jayme, Mountain Home, Arkansas
From Ghosts of America 2

. . . .

21.
The Ranch House

Valparaiso, Florida

I used to live in a rental ranch house in Valp, Florida. I always felt uncomfortable being there by myself. The first experience I had was one night when my boyfriend and I were watching late night TV. The TV turned off. I was on one side of the room lounging on a couch, and my boyfriend was opposite to me stretching out on the other couch. Against the wall and between us was a sofa chair. I see that the remote was sitting on the armrest of the empty chair. I picked it up, went to lie down, turned the TV back on and back to our show.

For some reason, when I turned it back on, instead of it being Channel 3 or what I was watching, it was the Weather Channel. Not even twenty seconds later it turned off again. The TV was the only light we were using. I turned it back on and stood directly in front of it. When I turned it on, it was a snow screen. Something cold turned my face to look out the window. I could see the snowy TV screen in the reflection. The shadow of a man's head neck shoulders and torso moved across the snow then disappeared! I screamed and ran out of the house.

Three weeks later--during Hurricane Ivan my roommate left town, but I decided to stick it out. The power went out for a week. The lights did not work, no AC. I was using candles for light and keeping all the doors and windows open for air flow. There was always this one spot in the bathroom hallway which was cold, very cold. My neighbor was having a grill out a block away, and my brother and his wife were going, so I thought I would too. The house was owned by my mom. My brother, his wife, and their two young children were the former occupants. I decided to mention what had happened to me and my boyfriend. As it turned out, my brother and his wife had some stories of their own.

Every month on the twenty-eighth in the middle of the night, their two young boys would come screaming into their bedroom that there was a man in their room looking at them. My brother's wife's brother was spending the night on the couch in the living room when he woke up because he could not breathe. He could not get up because something was standing on his chest. He slid out from whatever it was and ran outside and could breathe. The wife also said the cold spot in the bathroom hallway would be there some days but others not. My friend and I left the grill out and walked back home.

When we got there, all the candles were lit even though we purposefully put them out beforehand. And my collected artist book was lying open in the living room. The page it was on, the picture that it showed was a demon standing on a man's chest while he was sleeping, and he was choking him. The man looked quite like the brother-in-law. This bothered both of us so we decided to get some drink. We started to play cards on the couch. That was when we heard the crying. All the doors and windows were open. We could not tell where the sound was coming from. I swore she was crying outside. He swore otherwise. Then we both started swearing together and spent the night outside.

A month later I was taking a shower. All the doors were open, and my music was blaring. I was too scared otherwise to be alone with no music or TV or something. Something turned my music off. I yelled "hey! Is someone in my house?" I washed the soap off my face and turned around because I felt someone in the tub behind me. I looked into the face of an old man with cuts all over his neck and face, then he disappeared. I grabbed my bathrobe and ran out of the house.

Three nights later my boyfriend was spending the night. During the middle of the night, he woke up. He opened his eyes, stared at my nightstand, and my lamp turned on. He turned it off then went back to bed. I moved out the week after and have always been curious as to what sort of things have happened to the new family living there. I drive by it often hoping to see the man who once terrified me.

Submitted by Lydia, Valparaiso, Florida
From Ghosts of America 2

. . . .

22.

Ghost Locomotive

Waycross, Georgia

Forty years ago my friend was telling me that there was ghost locomotive that ran on the railroad by West Highway 84 on New Year's Eve at midnight every year. I said "nah, there is no ghost. " I joined him, and it was four boys and one girl in the car. The weather was perfectly calm and very cold with bright moonlight and not even a cloud. An older boy was driving on West Highway 84 out in the dark country, not too far. The driver was looking for a left turn on any block that would lead us to the railroad. We parked on a dirt road beside the railroad. There were just three minutes left before the ghostly locomotive would appear. We decided to stay in the car because it was so cold. We waited around and one of our friends hollered "there is small light over there!" Sure enough, I saw the light right above the railroad. It looked like real locomotive light, so I waited for the light to come close by where we were.

I saw the light that flew by us. What I saw was a light that looked like an old fashion lamp. It was like a light lid inside the glass cover. The light did not flick. It traveled very straight above the railroad. It did not go down or up or move from one side to another. It appeared to move at a steady and stable speed. I do not see an engine or any cars attached to it, except for the loud noise and vibes. This light lasted for less than ten seconds. While all this happened I also jumped out and looked out for any aircraft above in the sky. And there was nothing up there. I then looked down on the ground and glanced as I saw the wind rushing through the weeds nearby. Then everything turned quiet, no noise or vibes. I decided to walk to the middle of the railroad to see if anyone was pulling our legs. I remembered looking up at the moonlight and then at my watch. It was now 11 o'clock. I found nothing. I said to myself "yeah, it seems to be a real ghost locomotive. "

I later discussed this with my mother, and she said "yes, it happens once every year. And no one seems to know why it happens the way it does" I have thought of going back and take another look once in a while, but I have not had a chance go back and take another look. Now it has been forty years. Still I have been thinking of going back there. It will take me four hours to drive. I hope this long trip will be worth my time.

Submitted by Nicky, Waycross, Georgia
From Ghosts of America 2

. . . .

23

You Are not alone

Walterboro, South Carolina

The home I rent in Walterboro is not only home to me but three others that are not alive. I have lived here since 2002. During the fall the activity gets intense around here. Here are my stories. My master bedroom is one of the most active areas of the house. When I first moved in and did not have my bed frame put together yet, I had no choice but to sleep on my mattress in the middle of the floor. My husband and I both awoke around 3:00 am feeling like the other was holding us down. I screamed for my husband to get off of me, and he said he was pinned down by an unknown force and was asking for me to help. We could not sleep for the rest of the night. The second night, still sleeping on the floor, I felt a spot next to my right foot getting hotter and hotter. At the peak of the temperature on this spot, it was so hot to the touch my hand turned red as though it was burned. I was actually afraid the bed was catching on fire.

About two hours later, the closet door swung open for no reason at all. And it was pushed open with a great force. Some of the personal effects that I had placed in the closet started flying across the room. I had to duck for cover, so I would not get hit. Since then I have been awoken to something touching my face, a feeling of getting bitten (with temporary teeth marks), or my hair being pulled. All of these activities started heavily in the month of October and seemed to subside by mid November although never going away completely.

The next spirit in my house is a woman. She resides in the hall bathroom. Every child that comes into my home is either terrified of this bathroom or curious of it. The ones that are curious always go in and play "peek-a-boo" with her by pulling back the shower curtain and actually saying those words "peek-a-boo". If you walk down the hallway and approach the bathroom, your vision will sometimes go to black. It is as if you were walking through her, and you were in darkness and could not see a thing in front of you. She can be seen sometimes walking from the bathroom to the bedroom that is directly across the hall. One time when my husband hit the exact area of both these doors, a picture that was on the wall flew off its hinge and landed ten feet in front on him. He went to pick it up and put it back on the wall, and it was lifted from his hand and was thrown back down in the same place it was on the floor. We both looked at each other in amazement not believing what we had just seen. Needless to say, that picture never went back up.

In the bedroom she visits the closet door will sometimes slowly crack open by itself. We use this extra room as a recording studio since we have no children, and it is just us. We have often picked up Electronic Voice Phenomenon (EVP)'s of a woman's voice during recordings in which there are only all men present.

The last of the spirits in my home can be found in the kitchen and family room which are connected as an open floor plan. I am still unsure as to the gender of this spirit. You will see it in form of a light. I have only seen its true form once when I was sitting in the living room. The stove light in the kitchen is always left on; my husband and I were both in the same room together. The hood light reflects off the wall, and I saw a shadow of someone as if it were standing in front of the stove. As soon as I saw it, it was gone. Other than that, I always see lights floating around in both the living room and kitchen. They usually are close to the ceiling and can be followed. Once you see it and look, it moves to the next spot in your peripheral vision. Just like the woman in the hallway, I have seen the light appear right next to me. Once spotted, it knocked my vision out. It was as if a hood had been placed over my face. It lasted all of two seconds before it went away, and my sight returned.

Some other strange things have happened, but we are unsure if it is different spirits or the three in the house. We leave the hall bathroom light on while we sleep at night for security reasons. You can see the shadows of feet under our bedroom door as if they were pacing up and down the hallway. You can also see a light that floats from the master bedroom to the front door. And last of all, sometimes you will hear knocking on the bedroom front and back door that vary in intensity when there is nobody there. A couple of times the doors have been hit so hard; I thought someone had broken into my home and was trying to break into my bedroom. I grabbed my gun, opened the bedroom door and searched the entire house to shoot the intruder, but nobody was there except me, frightened and shaking like a leaf in the wind. And there were no signs of entry, forced or unforced.

My husband and I have found all of these very curious. These have caused us to venture into the unknown by doing paranormal investigations on our home and other locations. I have caught EVP's, photographic mists/apparitions, and strange temperatures or Electro-Magnetic Field (EMF) readings in these sites. We have no intentions on leaving this home and have found that our faith in the lord will protect us from any further physical harm. For personal reasons, I wish not to divulge my precise location in Walterboro. If any other families out there are experiencing the same situation as mine, you are not alone. Keep your faith and ask for god's help.

Submitted by Angela, Walterboro, South Carolina
From Ghosts of America 2

. . . .

24.

Now A Believer

Port Charlotte, Florida

I moved into my house in Port Charlotte, Florida in December 2009. The weather was nice and cool, so I did not bother closing the back door. I just locked the screen porch doors with the latch locks. I did not have cable yet, so I only had DVDs to watch. A couple of nights I fell asleep watching them and awoke to the awful feeling that someone was in the house with me, watching me. I was scared. I searched the house looking for an invader but never saw or found anybody or anything. I am forty-five years old and not much scares me.

Now my girlfriend has moved in with me. Well about mid April the weather was still very comfortable, and the back door was still being left open. My girlfriend kept telling me that at night while sitting out back on the porch in the dark she was seeing a dark shadow moving about the house. I was optimistic and not thinking about my previous "encounters". Well, one night about 2 o'clock in the morning I was already in bed just starting to doze off when she came running into the bedroom. She jumped into the bed quickly and latched herself onto me. When I asked her what was wrong she said she heard a noise behind her. It sounded like my knees do when I get out of bed. She, of course, was expecting to see me standing there when she turned around. She was instead looking into the dark laundry room, and she saw two glowing red eyes looking at her. She did a double-take look, but they were gone! That was when she came running to bed! Being half asleep I really was not too worried about what she had to say. The next day when she told me about it I could tell she was really scared.

When the end of May came, it started to get hot outside. Now the A/C was on, and the back door was closed and locked. We were lying in bed talking. It was about 1 o'clock in the morning, I was on my right side facing her looking toward the door. She was on her left side facing me. The bedroom was well lit from outside by the street light. When all of a sudden I actually saw someone look into the bedroom from the living room. All I saw was the top of the head. It looked down at us and then pulled back. Not wanting to freak her out, I did not say anything about it till the next morning. I was not too scared at that moment which was why I waited to tell her. Later that same night every time I looked up I expect to see it again but did not. Instead, once very late when I looked up I thought I saw an older woman about seventy years old. She was standing there in the bathroom doorway wearing a white dress with flowers on it. I blinked my eyes a couple of times, and she was gone. I have always been someone that had to see something to believe it. Well, now I am a believer. Guess we will just have to wait to see what happens next.

Submitted by Anonymous, Port Charlotte, Florida
From Ghosts of America 3

. . . .

25.
Who Were They?

Savannah, Georgia

In the summer of 2001 I worked as a camp counselor on Rose Dhu Island. The other camp counselors thought it would be funny to scare the girls by having me jump out on the trail during a night hike. It just so happened that the trail they wanted to walk the girls down was right through a part of the island where you could still see the trenches dug by Confederate troops. Rather than crouching down in the weeds for who knows how long, I decided I would sit in the dark by one of the log cabins waiting for the lights of the flashlights further down the wooded trail. It felt like I had waited there for hours, but it was probably no more than an hour in total. It was then that I saw a faint light coming up the secluded path. I got closer to the woods out of the open area and hid like I was supposed to. The closer the light got, the more I realized something was amiss.

First of all it was not a flashlight. I was seeing what looked like a lamp. I have seen electric lamps, and this did not look like an electric lamp. As the people got closer it became apparent that these were absolutely not girl scouts. Even right after the event had happened I professed that they were dark male figures walking towards me. I could not make any more of them out than that, but it was enough that I jumped out of the bushes and ran for my life back to the main building. I could hear people chasing me. At one point I even fell down which scared me to death because I fell at the edge of a field where I would be very visible in the moonlight. Gratefully the field was not far from the main building. I got there shaking and scared at what I had seen. We all decided it must have been people who came by boat (because the main road onto the island has a gate on it that you cannot pass through) to steal the crabs caught in our traps. However, I never understood why these grown men would have such an old-fashioned lamp rather than just using a more efficient electric one that can easily be picked up at any camping store nearby.

I wonder if they were a group of fishermen who chased me down in an attempt at not being caught, or they were a group of Confederates still ready and waiting to fight for their cause. When I calmed down the counselors informed me that they had chosen to take a different path and just assumed I had walked back when they did not show. They were not even on that part of the island that night, and no one was staying in those cabins that week. They were actually starting to get a little bit worried when I was not coming back because I was out there alone with no flashlight.

Submitted by Rachel, Savannah, Georgia
From Ghosts of America 3

. . . .

26.

My Parents' House

Valparaiso, Florida

My parents and I moved to Valparaiso from Eglin Air Force Base in 1988 when I was twelve. We bought a new house in Crystal Lake Estates. All was quiet around the house at first, but in 1998 things for me and my family changed. My son and I were living with my parent's while my husband was away at basic training in Alabama. It was the middle of April and my husband had only been gone since April 1st when things started to happen. I was awakened in the middle of the night by someone sitting at the foot of my bed. I could feel the pressure on my lower legs and feet. When I opened my eyes I saw what I thought was my mom looking at me, and I went back to sleep.

Even though I was twenty-two at the time my mom still came in every night to check on me and most of the time to turn off my TV. It was around 7:00 am when I got up that next morning, and the first thing I noticed was that my TV was still on. I immediately went to my parents' room after hearing my mom blow drying her hair. I walked in and asked her why she came into my room and sat at the foot of my bed just looking at me. She looked at me like I was crazy and said that she did not come into my room. I told her not to joke around and that it was not funny. She vehemently denied coming into my room. By this time my dad had woken up and wanted to know what we were talking about. So I asked him why he had come into my room, and just like my mom he said that he had not. My mother said that if he had gotten up it would have woken her up. They said that they slept really well last night. I looked at them both kind of panic stricken and began to realize that now they were beginning to worry.

There was no way it was my son, because he was only thirteen months old and still slept in his crib, and besides that I saw an adult looking at me. I told my parents exactly what I had seen and in the middle of our conversation I remembered that I could see my TV was still on through the person who was on my bed. I also realized that my TV was still playing when I woke up. I was not scared when I saw the person. It was looking at me so lovingly, and shortly after I opened my eyes I fell back to sleep. I never figured out who it was, but I think it was one of my relatives that had passed just coming to check on me now that my husband was away. But this one incident set the tone for what else has happened in my parent's house and what still goes on to this very day.

Submitted by DH, Valparaiso, Florida
From Ghosts of America 2

. . . .

27.

A Presence In Our Home

Rex, Georgia

Our house was haunted over a three-year period. A small girl lived in the upstairs. Sometimes you would see her out of the corner of your eye at the top of the stairs or in front of the window in the back of the house. She would interact with my kids by playing with their toys at night while they were sleeping. They would smell strawberry lip-gloss and see their toys left out even if the toys had been put away before they went to bed. They were just little mischievous activities.Then a darker presence began to visit. Some nights I would be up late working and the temperature would drop to the point that you would need to wrap in blankets. One evening I started to go to bed, and a dark stick figure was standing in my bathroom. At first I thought my eyes were playing tricks. However, the figure began to move toward me coming out of the bathroom walking around the end of my bed toward me. I was so afraid I just closed my eyes and began to recite the Lord's Prayer. In a few minutes the terrified feeling left me, and the room was clear. I could not talk about this for months because I was worried my kids would be too afraid.

We decided to sell the home. The people who purchased the home from us only lived there for about a year. One evening my daughter and I returned to our old neighborhood to visit our friends. We drove by our old home just to see if anyone had purchased it. I pointed my car lights into the large window in the kitchen. A dark figure walked through the kitchen while the lights were stationary in the window. I became terrified again and quickly drove away. I have never returned to the site because I am afraid the spirit might follow us to our new home.

Submitted by DLT, Rex, Georgia
From Ghosts of America 3

. . . .

28.

The Drums

Fort Benning, Georgia

We were living on Arrowhead Road at the time. I was woken up around 2:00 am the first time to the sound of what I could only describe as war drums, Native American drums. It sounded like it was far off. I lay in bed thinking of what it could be. A high school was down the road, but they would not be practicing at 2:00 am. It did not sound like someone with the bass to their music cranked up driving through the housing area. I woke up my husband to see if he could hear it. He did, but he said it was probably just someone with their music up loud. I put it out of my mind until about two weeks later when I heard it again. Only this time my husband was awake too, and he heard it. He said it sounded like war drums. I did not tell him that was what I thought until he told me. It sounded so far away, but you could definitely make out each time the drum was hit. The next morning I got up with my son to get him ready for school. I was outside watching the bus pick him up when my neighbor came out, and we talked for a minute. She asked me if I heard someone beating on a drum last night around 1:00 am. I said "you heard it too?" I was so glad that someone other than me and my husband heard it. She said "yeah, and it sounded far off like it was quite far away from us. " About a week after we heard the drums for the last time some Native American graves were discovered on the other side of post when earth was being moved in order to start new construction. Now there have been battles waged on Fort Benning property during the Civil War and probably some of the revolutionary war as well. It is also a huge area where the Cherokee once lived. I do not know what to think to this day, but at least I was not the only one who experienced it.

Submitted by DKH, Fort Benning, Georgia
From Ghosts of America 3

. . . .

29.
The House, The Garden, and The Lady
Flippin, Arkansas

When we were planning on moving to Flippin, we did house hunting like any normal family. We found an adorable little house near the school and immediately contacted the owner of the house. When we were finally allowed in, the man told us that the house had not been lived in since his mother passed away some forty years ago. I decided that while my parents were looking at the rent prices and their income I would look around. I walked aimlessly around the bedrooms. When I was walking out of the main bedroom, I felt something scratch me. I thought it was my little brother, so I wiggled my back a little and wailed out knowing my brother would follow me out. When I walked back in the living room where my parents were, my little brother was asleep in my dad's arms. I did not think anything of it and decided to walk outside and see the garden.

The outside was beautiful. It had bushes, flowers, vines, and trees. Everything was colorful. I have always had a soft spot for flowers. I love the color purple, so when I saw beautiful purple flowers poking out of the ground, I bent down and admired them. I reached out my hand to pick one. When my hand got close, it felt like someone was smacking my hand. I pulled away and looked around, but no one was there. I reached out again and plucked the flower from the ground. When I stood up, I felt like someone was kicking and punching my backside. When I turned around there was a black mist looking at me. I could make out a face, and it looked like an angry one. Absolutely freaked out, I did what I always do in nervous situations. I said "hi. " The face looked like it perked its ears, but the lips thinned. When I took a small step back, the mist disappeared. I walked back to the door and was about to walk in, when the same mist materialized. This time, I could hear a voice. "Leave!" it demanded. "Leave! Leave! " it chanted. I freaked out and ran inside and clung to my father for dear life.

When the man looked at me and asked if I liked the house, I asked him without hesitation if his mother who had died in the house. He looked hesitant, but said that she did die of a stroke. Later that day when we were leaving, I looked out to the garden again the same mist was there, standing next to the tree. It still looked mad, and I said a little prayer for the person who lived there next.

Submitted by Rachel, Flippin, Arkansas
From Ghosts of America 3

. . . .

30.
He Is Protective Of The Child

Niceville, Florida

My best friend and her son had moved into an income based duplex on Azalea Drive after her divorce. After she was settled in the stress of it all had her at her ends. Once afternoon her son who was not quite two at the time kept messing with the power button on the TV. After several warnings to him she grabbed him up, spanked him, and set him in time out on the couch.

There was a man that stayed there who became very protective of her son. He started to mess with the power button himself turning the TV on and off. She apologized for being so harsh to her son, and the TV was left off the rest of the night. A lot of times when her son got in trouble things would happen, for example, things would fly off the top of the entertainment stand and doors would bump.

A few times as she was folding laundry in her room she would notice out of the corner of her eye, him rush at her from the hallway then disappear. One morning around 5:00 am she was woken up by him standing at her bedroom doorway and just shaking his head, arms folded. She told him she had to wake up in a couple hours for her new job, and he left her alone. At one point her ex-husband had moved in. They were trying to work things out. The man did not like it, and her ex was woken several times being pinned to the bed and not being able to move. Eventually after things between them calmed down, so did the man. These are all stories she and her ex had told me.

Now with my own additions, being New Years Eve he hit the closet door being upset. Her son was not there, and I saw him walk into my friend's son's room when I was the only one in the house. He was about 5'10". He had brown hair, long and combed back. He had on him a white shirt tucked into khaki pants. We all believe he was just protective of the child. None of us ever felt truly threatened, but I never stayed the night there!

Submitted by Anonymous, Niceville, Florida
From Ghosts of America 3

. . . .

31.
In Our Dream Home

Macclenny, Florida

My husband and I have lived in Macclenny, Florida for seventeen years. We started building on our property our dream home. It was a log cabin in the woods! We had company and not the invited kind. I would love to get a ghost hunting professional opinion on what we thought was a haunting. I overheard my husband talking to one of his coworkers about people having a full length conversation upstairs. When he got to the top of the stairs it was quiet again! Nobody else was in the house! It had not happened just once but many times. I confronted him, he said he could not tell what they were saying, but he was quite sure they were in an in-depth discussion about something. My husband said he saw shadows as well as lots of banging noises.

Now that we have lived here in our new home for nine months something was setting off our smoke detectors playing games. So far nothing harmful has happened. The fire department could not explain why they just kept going off. We have about ten detectors in the house, and when one went off, they all went off! The list went on and on. We had tapping on the shoulder. Our daughter (who just turned sixteen) has had the side of her bed slapped hard enough to wake her up. That scared her pretty bad. Our son has seen shadows in his room. I saw a young woman with long brown hair behind me when I was cleaning his mirror. I ran out of his room. I would not go in there when alone in our house. The breaking point was when my dad was here to drop off a present for my daughter. He said while he was helping install our kitchen cabinets he would see things moving around the house out of the corner of his eye. He told himself it must just be the cat. That was the final straw! I would now love to get some help.

Submitted by Toni, Macclenny, Florida
From Ghosts of America 3

32.

The Gravity Of That Place

Fluker, Louisiana

As a young girl my family moved from Baton Rouge into a large old home off of Interstate 51 in Fluker. One side of the home had been previously burned down and rebuilt earlier. It sat on many acres that led deep into the woods where my sister and I would find arrowheads and even what seemed to be a small 'slave cabin' off to the side of the house. I am not sure of the history exactly, but I know we were not alone there. The constant feeling of being watched accompanied by strange sounds was just the beginning. My sister's room was part of the area that had been rebuilt. One day I came walking into the kitchen for a late afternoon snack when I saw out of the corner of my eye what I thought was my dad standing in front of the fridge. I opened a cabinet asking him what he was looking for. When I turned around, no one was there. I ran into my mother's room where she then told me that my dad was not even at home.

The attic was the entire second story of the house where we found old relics and antiques from the prior tenants of many years ago. It is said that spirits and energy can be found within such personal belongings. I was "pushed" onto an enormous pair of bull horns one day when my sister and I were exploring. Thank god she was there to catch me from being impaled. I never went back up there after that. A woman dressed in Victorian period type clothing was often seen at our home. Even my father who is a skeptic himself once told my mother in confidence that he awoke from a deep sleep to see the woman floating above him in bed (she later told my sister and me about this.) We would hear music such as a flute in the forest late at night when we were trying to fall asleep knowing that no one was anywhere near us by at least a mile or so.

One particular night my sister was dosing off to sleep when she heard a whisper in her ear. She jerked her head to see if anyone was there, but of course there was no one. She laid her head back on the pillow, and as soon as she closed her eyes she heard it louder and clearer. This time she heard "get out!" She jumped up out of bed and ran across the room to turn on the light. When she flipped the switch the room had a purple haze to it, and the light popped, burning out. She ended up sleeping in my room for the rest of the night. Eventually we moved out of the house, but still to this day I often wonder about it. I would love to know more about the history. I now live in Florida, but my grandparents still live in Fluker in Kent Acres. Whenever I go home for Christmas or to visit I am constantly being pulled by the gravity of that place.

Submitted by Kristen, Fluker, Louisiana
From Ghosts of America 3

. . . .

33.

Mysteries

This story comes from a lady I grew up with. She is one of the most honest people I know. She is like a grandmother to me. Her story happened in the later 1980s on River Road outside of Gilbert. She and a friend were out driving to a home one night. At the time she was driving a car. She had turned off of highway 572 and onto River Road. The two women had traveled down the road a little bit before noticing a bright white light hovering in the sky over the river. She slowed the car down and was staring in amazement at the light. Now on the river bank there was a man who lived there with his hunting dogs. He kept his dogs in cages along the bank. She said they could hear the dogs barking over her loud diesel engine, but they could not hear any other noises or any helicopter.

The light appeared to be quite large and descended below the treetops on the river. After a few seconds of hovering over the river water the light rose suddenly and shot off into the sky. The woman looked at her friend and her friend stared back at her. They could not believe what they had just seen. The two women went about with their business and made it to the house. I understand that that night the two ladies appeared to be "haunted" by a strange bright light in the sky. I believe everything from hauntings to UFOs. I believe they are related in some form of energy. Together we can take these stories and piece them together to form a more solid understanding of these mysteries.

Submitted by Jon, Gilbert, Louisiana
From Ghosts of America 3

. . . .

34.
The Devil House
Tuscumbia, Alabama

Back in February 1997 my then-husband and I bought a house on North Hook Street in Tuscumbia. We immediately felt a "presence" in the house, but since we were strong Christians we were not afraid. We moved into the house both excited to start our new life in our house, but within a week we were at each other's throats constantly. We began to hear footsteps walking through the house, knocking in the walls, and loud scary music every night when we went to bed. Once I went outside to find out which neighbor was playing the loud music, but there was no sound outside. It was perfectly quiet out there. The music was coming from inside the house, but there was no radio, TV, or stereo on. We heard crashing sounds like boxes falling at the other end of the house, but when we would investigate everything was in place. We heard a large pipe fall onto the floor in the basement, but when we went down there we found that it had not fallen.

Most of the sounds we heard, other than the ones we heard nightly when we were in bed, only got worse when we began to paint. That was when we would hear things falling, and my then-husband heard a little girl's voice which usually called out his name. The only time I heard a voice was one morning when I was in the shower at about 5:30am. I heard a very loud man's voice, and it made me angry because I thought my then-husband was up and had the TV on which I thought would wake my daughter. I hurried to get out of the shower and still heard the loud voice. When I opened the bathroom door the voice stopped. The TV was off, and everyone else in the house was asleep. There was also a terrible odor that would come and go. Sometimes it was so bad you could not stand to go into the bathroom. One evening while standing at the kitchen sink washing dishes something in the dining room caught my eye. I turned toward it, and I saw a light human-shaped "mist" standing there. It was probably a little over six feet tall with no features. It was just a misty figure. It slowly moved toward the bedroom. I went into the dining room then looked all throughout the house and did not see it anymore. Anytime we walked through a dark room in the house especially the kitchen we could feel a spirit near. You had to walk all the way across the kitchen to turn on the light, and it always felt like someone was running up on me before I got to that light switch.

We also had things "disappear. " If you were using a pen and had put it down for a second, it would be gone when you went back to find it. One night we had moved the furniture around in the living room, and my then-husband was sitting in his chair looking at the wall opposite him. He said "oh my god! Do you see that?" I went over to where he was and looked at the wall and there was the face of the devil. It was in the plaster. It was like the face of a goat, but in one of the eyes was a pentagram. It totally freaked us out. I ran and got some sand paper but could not take it all off. I got some spackling compound and put a lot of it on the wall. After I sanded it down, I painted it, and you could not see it anymore. We never forgot that it was there, on the front wall of the living room.

We had our pastor come over and bless the house, but nothing changed. We (mostly I) would bind the spirits' works in our home and command them to leave. They would settle down, but as soon as he and I would have a cross word, they were right back. We finally got so frustrated that we got more help. We had asked three pastors, a minister of music, and a few more strong Christian men to come over one night for a "house-cleansing. " I cleaned the house and got ready for our "house-cleansing. " The house was going crazy. We had been hearing noises almost non-stop since the previous afternoon. The odor in the house was so embarrassing. We had candles burning and windows open, but still it was sickening! We prayed, confessed sin, and then we began to go through the house showing the men anything that could be connected to anything sinful. Those included books, movies, albums, CDs, tapes, even my black clothes which they said probably had ties to the occult. The man who owned the house before had left wine and whiskey bottles stashed all up under the house. All these things went into the back yard and a huge fire was built with these things. They went through the house praying and anointing it with oil. When one of the guys went into the bathroom and anointed it commanding the spirits to leave, the odor disappeared! He started yelling "it was a spirit! It's gone!" The odor was gone. That night was the first night since we had bought the house almost a year before that we slept easily. The house felt clean, and we did not hear a sound.

However, as soon as we began to argue it started all over again. We heard knocking in the walls. We heard footsteps walking through the house right up until the day we moved out in September of 1998. The house was built on land that bordered an old cemetery which had been moved years before. After researching the situation it is my belief that the land could not be cleansed because of the cemetery. There might have been bodies that were not moved. The homes that were built there might have been built on top of those bodies or land where they had been put to rest. On April 9, 2009 I went back to that house to ask the current residents if they had had any experiences like the ones we had. No one came to the door, so I left a note. I left and went to my dad's house and found him dead. I am not saying there is a connection between the two things. My dad was sick, and I knew he would not make it much longer. However, I have not had the nerve to go back to what we call "The Devil House."

Submitted by Kitten, Tuscumbia, Alabama
From Ghosts of America 5

. . . .

35

Mr. Ghost

Longwood, Florida

I live in the Sweetwater Springs subdivision located on the west side of Longwood, FL next to the Wekiva River and Wekiva State Park. My home was completed in early 1989 as a spec home. It sat vacant for a while and then became a rental for a year. We bought the house in mid-1990. Soon after moving in I occasionally began to see a fast moving shadow. I have healthy skepticism, so I did not say anything about it at first. For one thing, the shadows moved very fast. So it was hard to be sure exactly what I saw. Secondly, the shadows were translucent. I could see through the human form that "grayed out" what was in the back of it. However, I could not see much detail.

Over the last twenty-four years we have gotten to know our "Mr. Ghost," as we call him, quite well. He has become far more adept at communicating, and my wife and I have become more capable of sensing him when he is around. He does come about half the time when we call him although if there are people visiting that he does not know, he keeps his presence (assuming he is there) clandestine. The beginning of significant events began when I saw a large, bright-white "ball of light" that hovered in mid air right in my path, not more than ten feet away. When I saw it, I heard (not with my ears but with some other pathway) a voice say "It's fine that you know I'm here, but it's best we don't communicate. " It was a firm and fatherly (but, not stern) voice (almost instructional.) As soon as it had delivered the mail, it whooshed away. That was about sixteen years ago.

Since then Mr. Ghost has learned to make white noise over the intercom when he is upset if a family member has been away for a long time. He would turn lights back on that I have turned off. He has cut down a set of venetian blinds (these were easily ten feet across) held by six nylon cords. The cords were cut so cleanly. I do not think I could have done as well with a scalpel. He can turn on, or turn off, the cable box and surround sound amplifier. For some reason he does not bother to turn on the actual TV. Maybe as long as the cable is on, he does not need the actual TV? I have no idea. Usually he is most active (he often wakes me up, I think for nothing more than to have some company) at 3:00 am to 3:30 am. He has moved a pen, three times in a row (within about a minute) off of a level counter top. The pen had a pocket clip on it, so it could not roll at all.

One night (this was just about two weeks ago) I was in bed watching TV with my wife sleeping next to me. All the lights were off, and the only light in the room was from the TV. I sensed Mr. Ghost was standing at the door of the bedroom, and I waved to him and went back to watching TV. A minute or so later he got my attention again, and I waved to him again and said "you can come in. " For whatever reason, he rarely comes into our bedroom and prefers to stay at the west end of our house. I went back to watching TV, and about ten seconds later, wham! It felt like a St. Bernard had hit the side of the bed at a full gallop. The king-sized bed really shook, and you could hear the impact over the TV. I guess I am used to him because I just laughed. Obviously I was not paying the attention to him that he was looking for.

There are so many instances, and so many different things he has done over twenty-four years. We are not scared of him, but we do take notice when he reaches out because usually it means he is upset about something. At first we had no idea. But now, we think that whenever one of us is away for a long time, especially if it is my autistic son, he gets very concerned. When my older children were in high school, if they came home late, as soon as they walked in the door, they used to feel what they described as "spider webs" all over their face and neck. No matter how they rubbed, the feeling would not go away. I do not know whether he was admonishing them or hugging them. I suspect it was the former.

I have had lots of cats and two dogs. They have not seemed to have reacted to him at all. Either they are used to him or they do not sense him. I cannot tell you for sure which it is.

Well, there is a lot more to tell, but this is too long already. We feel as though he is a part of our family, and frankly if he left, we would be saddened.

Submitted by DCG, Longwood, Florida
From Ghosts of America 6

. . . .

36.
Cursed Gift

Thomasville, Georgia

I live in a small trailer park in the county in Thomasville. I have heard what sounds like a TV or radio playing inside my house, but I do not even have a TV, and the only radio is beside my bed. My neighbor has experienced the same in her house. Sometimes it feels like my bed is shaking. Sometimes more violently than others, and sometimes it feels like there is something big moving around beneath my bed pushing and sliding around on the underside of my mattress. The same neighbor said they have felt an uneasy feeling in one of their bathrooms, and it feels like something is shaking the toilet from time to time. There have been times during the night and early hours of the morning, I have seen what looks like a person moving very quickly.

Three days ago I left my house to walk to the neighbors, and they were with me. At the end of my house it looked like someone was standing in the window. I only caught a glimpse and turned to run as I thought someone was in my home. My daughter was with me and saw this also, except she gave a more detailed description of what she saw. She said it was a girl in a white dress with blue eyes and long curly blond hair. I immediately told her to wait outside while I checked the house. I took my dog inside with me. I checked everywhere that someone could be or hide. There was nobody there. When I went to the room that I saw someone in the window of, there was only one thing amiss. There was a wooden cross that had been hanging on the wall at the head of the bed, and I found it off the wall. It was lying at the end of the bed. I know it was hanging sturdy, and there was no way it could have just fallen down.

Neighbor also said she knew that at some point in time someone committed suicide in her home. I have been trying to search through property records, but it is hard when it is a mobile home, and addresses have changed through the years. I do not know what we saw, or what the noises we are hearing are all about. I hope I do not ever see anything like that again! It scared me so much I ran and tripped over a wheel barrel handle in my neighbor's back yard, sending me flying for a loop. I had pretty bad bruise on my leg, hit my head, and injured my back. Regretfully, this probably will not be the only post I make.

This "problem" seems to have been with me for as long as I can remember. Things got so bad in one of my homes; I called in Paranormal Investigators. I was not happy with the end result. Their psychic medium told me I am a psychic medium, and so are my children. That it runs in bloodlines. My mother and my grandmother were the same way, but they were able to suppress it. I am not. I was basically told your house is not haunted; you are. He explained that many people with those kinds of abilities in one house makes it a lighthouse for spirits, good and bad. They know who can see and hear them and will come to you if you can see/hear them. Some call it a gift; I say it is the gift that is a curse. I do not want to hear and see these things!

Submitted by D, Thomasville, Georgia
From Ghosts of America 6

. . . .

37.
Small Forgotten Souls

Wellborn is now a small quiet town in northern Florida. Once it was larger than its sister towns to the east, Lake City and to the west, Live Oak. However, what most people around these parts do not know is it has the most graveyards of either Lake City or Live Oak. Most of these cemeteries are now just places of sandy dirt, markers no longer readable and rotten flowers. Several years ago I had taken a back road home and come across one of these forgotten cemeteries. I was amazed as to where it was - right off of busy Highway 90 and just west of Wellborn. I had been by here dozens of times and never noticed it.

Something about this shaded moss covered spot made me want to stop. I got out of my car and walked through the gate. A feeling of immediate sadness and heaviness came over me. But something told me to keep going. I briefly looked at tombstone after tombstone and felt such sorrow at the young ages, infants, one year old, two and eight year old twins. No one in the cemetery seemed to be over twelve. I also noticed the last burial was 1864. I finally made it to the back of the fenced in area, and there a huge tree had fallen over several graves. I stood there thinking how sad this neglected cemetery was. It was obvious the only visitors this cemetery had were drunken ones. I started to turn and leave when a noise made me turn to the back again. Part of me wanted to run and part of me said I had been watching horror movies too long. There through the trees on a bright sunny Florida day was a misty, white form. I stood frozen in my tracks as whatever it was floated away. I could not get out of that cemetery fast enough!

Once I got home I recruited my husband to go back with me to check it out again. The second time through the gate I did not have the heavy feeling. We walked to the back and looked around. There outside the fence barely noticeable was a grave and a small wooden grave marker that had grown into a tree. The writing on it was not legible, but if you were not looking for it, you would not notice it. I have no idea who was buried outside this fence, perhaps a slave. We will never know, but even the lost need prayers.

Submitted by Mary, Wellborn, Florida
From Ghosts of America 1

. . . .

38.
Special Wing

One of my close friends had recently moved into an affordable studio apartment in Fayetteville Arkansas. This newly renovated building was once a rehabilitation center years ago, but had now been converted into a studio apartment complex by the new owners of this property. My friend had been given a room in a wing of this complex where he had heard that no one had occupied it for quite some time. Although he found this to be a bit strange the monthly price was just too good to pass up. Besides, he preferred to have some peace and quiet over a busy apartment wing. He gladly opted to becoming the only person living down this particular wing of studio apartments.

On his first night of sleeping in this studio apartment he was awakened at 4:00 am sharp by what appeared to him as a fairly thin pale looking elderly woman in a nightgown who was sitting on his chest while at the same time pressing down hard on him with her finger on the side of his neck. As he attempted to get up from the bed he noticed that the lady kept pressing upon him so forcefully that he could not physically get up on his own. As shocked as he was, he quickly recalled that as a child he had been told by his church going parents that if he ever came across any serious danger to simply call out on god's name. As he tried uttering god's true name the apparition quickly vanished before his eyes. Still shaken up by what had just occurred, he then was able to get up out of bed and examined his neck in the bathroom mirror only to find his neck a deep red color and feeling very sore from where this apparition had kept pressing upon him with its appendage. A few hours later he left for work and decided to take the strange occurrence as just a bad nightmare.

On the second night in this apartment he was again awaken with the feeling of a strange presence of someone or something being in the same room with him. Almost immediately after waking up he also heard what sounded like a small child running up and down the wing outside of his apartment. It sounded like the child kept opening and closing every door in this wing as he passed by. He promptly rushed to open the door, and there was no sign of anyone down the hall at all. Upon returning to his bed, he heard the sink faucet running in his bathroom. He urgently rushed over to see why his bathroom faucet had turned on all on its own. He found no one there, and the sink faucet turned fully to the off position. Out of curiosity he then decided to touch the bowl of the sink and found fresh water still around it. As late as it was, within a few hours he again proceeded to get ready for work and thought nothing of this second strange occurrence in the apartment.

On his third night of sleeping in this apartment he was again awakened by what he described as someone scratching the walls inside his room. The scratches appeared to slowly get louder and come closer to where his bed was situated. And once again, he felt a strange presence in this room, but he saw no one visibly there. He was now so scared to the point that he curled up entirely under his bed sheets for the remainder of the night. Eventually, the noises stopped and he headed off to work once more. That day after work he called the apartment manager of this complex and asked to be moved to another apartment wing altogether as he related these strange occurrences to her as well. The apartment manager told him that even though she did not believe in these types of things; oddly enough she had received similar complaints from a previous tenant who had also experienced more or less the same things he had and who also asked to be moved to another wing.

Submitted by Anonymous, Fayetteville, Arkansas
From Ghosts of America 2

. . . .

39.
They Are Welcome.

Titusville, Florida

I have lived here in Titusville for nearly three years now. I feel there is someone or something in my home. I live close to Indian River and the Enchanted Forrest. I know quite a bit about the history here. This fact leads me to believe that I am probably not the only one who will say they have had strange occurrences in their home. Here is my story.

My boyfriend often travels for his job. Before leaving on one of his trips we decided to buy a fifty-inch flat screen TV. Well, a day or so after he had left for work the TV had cut off, just the TV, and not the cable or surround sound that is all controlled by one remote. I would turn it back on and within a couple of hours it would cut off. This would happen no more than twice in a day. It did not happen every day, but it seemed to always happen when he was not at home.

I also experienced a bowling ball sized bright light in my bedroom. Around 4:00 am in the morning while I was sleeping I had this eerie feeling that I was being watched. I opened my eyes and saw a bright white light in front of me. It was impossible to have a light that bright in my room because it was still dark outside and I have also placed black paper over my windows in my room, so it would not heat up during the day. I could not explain the light because there was no way for a light that bright to be in my room at that time in the morning.

I have felt someone or something tugging on pants and when I turn around, nothing is behind me. I have a picture of my grandmother, who has passed, on one of my bookshelves, and it was turned around. I mean completely turned around. That cannot be explained either. I do not mind if there is someone or something here in my home because they are not bothersome, and

109

I actually welcome them. For anyone who is out there and believe that they might have spirits, I say this "you are not alone and believe."

Submitted by A, Titusville, Florida
From Ghosts of America 2

. . . .

40.

Ghost Enthusiasts

Statesboro, Georgia

Two separate real estate clients of mine told me about two separate incidents while they lived in Statesboro, Georgia. One told me about a dirt road that college kids would drive down at night to see a shadow figure of a man they said you would swear was digging in the middle of the road with a shovel. One night, they got out of their car, which was parked in the middle of the road with its head lights still on. They all saw the apparition digging. They were all arm in arm and slowly walking toward the figure when it stopped digging and turned toward them. Of course, they all freaked out and ran.

In another incident, a client told me that one mid-week evening after 10:00 pm or so, he and his girlfriend at the time were returning home to a house in which he rented a room. He said the house had parking in the back, and you had to drive under a little stone drop off area or portico. Sitting there on the outside wall of the drop off, facing away from the house, he saw a young girl about ten or eleven wearing older period clothing. She had long blonde hair. He said his first inclination was to ask why she was out so late on a school night and he wondered where her parents were. He parked his car within seconds and immediately got out and turned in the girl's direction, and she was gone. He then said out loud "where did she go?" That was when his girlfriend said "you saw her too?". They were both convinced they saw a spirit of some sort.

He is a university police officer now here in Georgia. I have never seen or experienced a ghost that I know of, but I hear so many stories like this from otherwise rational sane people. Makes me go hmm... And feel jealous. My main ghost goal is to find truly haunted places in Georgia and visit them with other enthusiasts I have come to know simply by bringing up the subject form time to time at work or at social gatherings. Seems like more people than not have some credible story. Know of any places in or around GA that are for real and not just some silly spooky place?

Submitted by Joe, Statesboro, Georgia
From Ghosts of America 2

. . . .

41.
Denial or Disbelief

Clermont, Florida

I live in an apartment complex located in South Clermont. Two days into my complete transfer to this apartment I was alone in the apartment with my one-year-old son vacuuming the carpets and steaming the rooms. When I was steaming one of bedrooms I felt a quick breeze in my hand as if someone had opened a freezer and quickly closed it. I totally ignored it and just went room by room checking what needed to be repaired to give a written report to the office. About four days after we painted the apartment and put things away. That same night my thirteen-year-old son came running screaming "Mom! Mom! My closet door was opened, and it closed by itself. " I told him it was probably air pressure from inside the closet or something. I again ignored it and dismissed it.

The next day I took some pictures when I was in the kitchen to show my apartment to some of my friends. One of the pictures I took of my son and husband showed the kitchen floor and something that looked like a black stain. I quickly looked at the floor to see the stain, but there was no stain. I showed it to my husband, and he said "that looks strange. " I thought maybe it was the reflection from the kitchen light. I turned off the light and took another picture from the same spot that the other picture was, and it showed it again. We both said "how weird it was," but we did not put much mind to it.

The next day my kids and I were playing with our dog when suddenly the dog stopped and stared towards the kitchen. He began to bark and would not stop. He later pulled back as if whatever he was barking at was coming near him. Few days passed and I was in the living room cleaning, and in the corner of my eyes I saw a black shadow pass by fast. It looked as though it was coming out of my bedroom. I told my husband and he said he

113

saw something like that before and thinking it was me. He never told me because he did not want me to be scared.

One night I was vacuuming one of our son's room (the same room that I had felt the cold breeze in my hand.) By the edge of the carpet and the wall under his desk I found a small plain female's wedding band in silver I had never seen before. I went to show my husband the ring and then called my fourteen-year-old son and questioned him. He said it was not his, and I doubt that it was his because the ring was very small. I kept the ring and hid it away. The next day I went to organize my five and thirteen-year-old sons' closets in their rooms. When I picked up one of my sons' sneakers another silver ring fell out. I felt speechless and mind bobbled because this ring looked like the other ring I found prior.

However, this one was thicker and for a male, but I assume it was a wedding band set to the other ring. I showed my husband, and this time I questioned my two oldest kids (my fourteen and thirteen-year-old sons). It was neither of them. The male wedding band was so small it did not fit any of them. I told my husband "let's take pictures with my camera phone everywhere in the apartment. I heard if there is something in here, sometimes it would show in the pictures. " I turned the lights off room by room and took pictures. First, we viewed one of the pictures I took of our younger sons' room, and there was a black stain that looked like the one in the kitchen floor. Then we viewed our oldest son's room. By one wall there was something that looked like a black hole. In my bathroom the picture showed three very dark small circles on the edge border of the wall and the top that were invisible when looked at.

For a few weeks nothing happened. We did not take any pictures or followed up with this. However, one day I was sitting in the living room, and I could swear I saw a black shadow taller than me. I thought it was my son behind me, so I said his name, and asked him to pass me a water bottle. Then I saw my son coming

114

out of his room. My heart beeped like I just had finished running a mile, and my adrenaline kicked up. I asked my son although I knew it was not him "were you just behind me?" Of course he said "no". I was in disbelief because this shadow was in a perfect form. I told my husband, and he said not to pay attention to that.

During this week day we met a guy through some friends. He participated in a ghost hunting show in Kissimmee. It so happened that he and his family had just moved into this very same complex we live in. He told my husband and I how he was on that ghost show. His wife said she did not believe in ghost, and so I said "neither do I. " Then we went on talking about the history of this complex. I was told that prior owners were not running this place properly and safely and that there was no security on this ground.

Later this complex was closed and condemned by the state because of the awful things that were happening. They said the owners did not take any actions to stop or prevent it. People were killed, stabbed, and shot in here. One woman was shot, and she ran to the office for help and dropped there and died. We also talked about how changed this place is now that it was bought by new owners and how good it is to have security officers.

Our new friend commented how he was in the ghost show, and my husband said "well, I believe in ghosts. " Then I told him what we were going through. A friend who lived next door mentioned how she was sitting in her living room, and she felt a cold breeze through her neck. Her hair was slightly pulled. Our new friend told us that we should get a recorder and just set it over night; let it record.

One day after strange things in our place had stopped for a while my husband was sitting in the living room watching TV. He told me that he heard a low tone voice behind the couch. The voice behind him said "hey. " He thought it was me, so he turned and looked behind, but nothing was there. I cannot explain what this is either. We are in denial, and we just want to let it be. Whatever is happening, I thank god it has not turned violent on us.

Submitted by Just, Clermont, Florida
From Ghosts of America 3

. . . .

42.

The Urn

Clearwater, Florida

Not too long ago while I was living on Redington Beach my husband purchased a silver urn at a yard sale along with some other items. The person he bought this from did not know where it came from or its history. It was quite beautiful and disturbing at the same time. It had two carved arms with animals and rams horns. Similar to old European hunting pictures or one of those old beer steins. It also had a liner inside the urn that was stained dark. He cleaned and polished it, and it was quite stunning and very heavy. He could not clean the liner so he threw it away. He laughed and said it had probably be used for some type of sacrifice.

We had no real use for it, so it sat on a shelf in our dinning room. Around that same time weird things started happening around our house. The dog would bark at things that were not there. Rooms would grow cold, and things would fall off shelves or go missing. Then one night our son who was about two at the time woke up and started crying. When we went to his room he could not be calmed down and was pointing. We saw nothing and chalked it up to a bad dream. This started to be a habit of waking and being scared for no reason. Once he was removed from the room he would settle down and go back to sleep. Then one night while I was home alone with the baby, the dog was barking, and the baby was crying, and someone was knocking at the door. I went to the door and called out, and no one answered. I looked through the peep hole, and no one was there. I picked up the phone and called my husband. While I was on the phone asking him to come home the phone went dead. I was standing in the dining room rocking the baby and happened to look over at the shelf where the urn sat. It looked like it was glowing. I thought it must be reflecting an outside light from somewhere.

117

Shortly after My husband came home and I told him what I had seen. He walked around the property and found nothing out of place. He picked up the urn and held it to the window. Nothing. There was no glow or anything unusual. I thought I was going crazy. The next day I told a friend what had happened. He went on-line to look up urns with the description of the one my husband had purchased. He found that ones similar to what we had indeed been used in sacrificial ceremonies around the 1800s. I told my husband we should sell the urn. I did not want it in the house any more. It was solid silver, and he could probably get a good price for it. The next day my friend who had found the information for me died suddenly of heart attack.

My husband took the urn to the back yard and started smashing it with a sledge hammer. It would not break easily. The strangest thing happened. It started to smoke and he kept hitting and hitting it. He took all the pieces and buried them somewhere in the woods of Fort Desoto Park. There was a burn mark left in the grass where he had destroyed the urn. All the strange things stopped after that. We did not stay in that house much longer, and we never disclosed what had happened there to the new owners. So if you bought a house on Redington Beach in the last twenty years, and you think it is haunted it just might be.

Submitted by Beach Dweller, Clearwater, Florida
From Ghosts of America 4

. . . .

43.

Lucy

Conway, South Carolina

I lived in Myrtle Beach, South Carolina in 1995 to 2000 and was a student at Coastal Carolina University. My friend Chuck asked me to go see a ghost with him one night. I declined and told him to inform me the next day with results, and I would be convinced to go myself. The following day he told me I had to go see this. About eight of us left together at about midnight and proceeded to check this out. I was told by the two girls that this ghost's name was Lucy, and she would come looking for her baby sometimes. Apparently her baby was kidnapped and abducted back in the Civil War and she came to find the baby carrying a lantern at her side. We drove down some country road. We took a right on a dark narrow dirt road and came to a stop about twenty yards short of a little bridge. It was a bridge with about a six-foot drop off each side. We parked our three cars on the right hand side and got out. As we walked to the bridge I began to ask questions. I had hoped to see this, so I was intuitive and curious. I had convinced myself that I would stand my ground to have an encounter with this so called ghost named Lucy.

Twenty minutes went by, and all of the sudden a light appeared well down the road. I was sure it was a car's headlights. We waited patiently. The light went off to the right into the woods then to the left. Then it began to come closer to us on the road's path. Once it got about fifty yards from us my mind began to race. I was skeptical, scared, and curious. At this point the light was so bright it was almost blue. To be honest it was the most beautiful thing I had ever seen. This light was projecting any light elsewhere like a normal flood light would, and the sound was amazing. It was hard to explain, but I was captivated and fascinated. My mind was not yet grasping what my eyes were seeing at this point. I was still trying to prove my eyes wrong thinking this had to be a bad prank or something. As the light got closer I was able to make out her silhouette. Her hair was in a bun, and she was carrying a glowing orange lantern at her side. She was wearing a dress tight at the waist, and it bowed out to her feet. She was not walking but more like gliding along. Needless to say I did not live up to my once bravery and actually was the first one of eight to start running. I was told not to run. I stopped, and we all walked quickly backwards to the vehicles. The girls were literally crying and we were all in a panic. As we all shuffled into our vehicles we kept a close eye on her (the ghost.) At this point she was now standing on the bridge we were just on. She leaned over the bridge. Meanwhile in the car my driver was hysterical, and I eventually got her in the back seat and I jumped in the driver' seat. We were in a Bronco parked in between the other two cars. We did not know it at the time, but our friend in front of us could not get her keys in the ignition. We were all screaming "Go! Go! Go!". Still watching as this pandemonium was going on. "Lucy" started heading steadily towards the car in front of us. When she reached the hood of that car which was only a car length in front of us my friends got their headlights on, and there was nothing in sight. We jumped out looking everywhere and anywhere. We found nothing.

We went back the next day to see what was back there. It was pretty much nothing but a long dirt road, an old small cemetery, and I think an abandoned house. Mind blowing to say the least! I still have lots of questions, but unfortunately I will probably never get the answers I am looking for.

Submitted by Jeremy, Conway, South Carolina
From Ghosts of America 5

. . . .

44.

Strange Feeling

Prairie Grove, Arkansas

I have always had the ability to see and hear things others could not. When I was twenty my husband and I lived with his parents in a small house on County Road 206. This place was eerie, and I had so many experiences there. I heard footsteps when no one else was home. Rushing out of my room thinking someone had broken in, I found the doors and windows were all locked, and nobody was there. I would wake up at night hearing voices outside our bedroom window not really being able to hear what they were saying. My husband never heard anything. He is a seriously heavy sleeper. I was outside playing with my infant daughter when I saw a man I did not know standing next to the house. When I looked at him he turned and walked behind it. I went to ask him if he needed something, and in the two seconds it took me to run around there he was gone. I searched all around the house, in the house, scanned the woods, (though in two seconds it would have been impossible for him to have gotten into the woods) and checked inside. I would get the feeling of being watched or followed around the house.

A couple of things I did not personally experience happened to my mother-in-law. One day (long before I moved in) she was looking for the deed to the house, and she had searched the house all day long. She could not find it anywhere. She was about to give up when she heard a woman say "it's in the pink bag in the closet. " Knowing there was not a pink bag in her closet, she went to the closet in the other bedroom and dug until she reached the bottom of a pile. There was a small pink purse with the deed folded up inside it. One night after my husband and I moved out she and my father-in-law were lying in bed when they heard people running around outside. My father-in-law went to investigate, but nobody was outside. They went back to bed, but the sound continued. Then they began hearing people shouting "hurry! Hurry up, please. They're burning!" and "get some more buckets! " and a woman screaming. My mother-in-law did some research on the property. She found out that around the time of the Civil War a family lived on the property, and their house was set on fire. Some family members made it out, but the man's wife and two of his children did not. The entire family was buried in a cemetery just up the hill from the house.

On Highway 265 leading out to Hogeye there is an open field next to a garage (it used to be called Boyz Under Tha Hood.) I would always get a feeling of dread and sadness when we drove past it heading to see his parents'. My husband asked me one day why I always shivered when we drove by there, and I told him the truth. I told him "I feel like someone is buried there who is not supposed to be. " He told me I was crazy. Fast forward a couple of months, we were sitting in my in-law's living room, and my mother-in-law who researches and documents cemeteries for the state started talking about a cemetery they found in a field just down the road. My husband looked at me funny, and his mom asked what was wrong. I asked her if it was the field next to the garage, and she said "yes, it was. " She asked how I knew. I told her that I would get that eerie feeling that someone was buried there that should not be. She gasped and her eyes went wide. She proceeded to tell us that it was an old family cemetery, but someone was buried there that did not belong with the family. A man was arrested in Fayetteville for murdering his wife and died in jail awaiting his hearing. They had nowhere else to bury him, so they put him in that cemetery.

My husband while still not completely a believer does not question when I get strange feeling as much anymore. I have so many more experiences in so many more different towns, but I will save them for another day.

Submitted by Tiffani, Prairie Grove, Arkansas
From Ghosts of America 6

45.
Before Moving On
Indian Lake Estates, Florida

Around the summer of 2006 my husband and I moved into a rental house on one of the canals that go out to the lake. My landlord had just purchased this home from a man who was eager to sell his parents' property since it was entrusted in his care while his elderly mom was in a nursing home. The landlord went through and told us what he wanted to keep. Part of our deal was to clean out the house and use or keep whatever we thought was still useful. It was so strange going through someone's belongings, but it gives you idea of who they were. I went through receipts, paystubs, pictures, furniture, and lots of garbage. So I knew the names of the previous owners that lived there.

We had lived there for a few months, and everything was quiet. It was very quiet out there. One day (and I remember it like yesterday) I was alone at home having a day off to do my chores. I went to my bedroom to fold laundry on my bed when I just got this feeling that I was being watched. As I was folding, in my peripheral vision I could see a shadowy figure standing in the hallway. When I looked up no one was there. I continued to ask if someone was there and looked around, but I did not get that feeling or see anything again. This still gives me chills when I recall it. About two days later as I was exiting the gated community I saw on the billboard that there was a memorial service for "Adele" the lady who lived in the house before me. I think she was just checking out the house before she went on to her next home.

Submitted by Jess, Indian Lake Estates, Florida
From Ghosts of America 6

. . . .

46.

The Ghostly Beach Comber
Isle Of Palms, South Carolina

This strange encounter happened on the beach near 21st Avenue. I am curious to know if anyone else has had a similar experience they would like to share. I grew up on the Isle of Palms several blocks north of the Front Beach Pier. Last week I was visiting my folks and decided to walk back from the Windjammer, one of the finest drinking establishments in the Charleston area. So there it is, make of this what you will. It was late (around 1:30 am on February 22nd, 2014) and let us just say I was one satisfied customer.

The beach was deserted with a slight breeze around fifty degrees and mostly clear skies. Passing under the pier I stopped to take a photo of the half-moon shining down on the calm ocean waves. A little ways past the pier I could see the dark shape of someone up ahead strolling toward me. The figure was contrasted by the moonlit white sand and was traveling in my direction about halfway between the shoreline and the sand dunes. I was walking close to the water, so it seemed we would be passing at a comfortable distance. Just then I began to feel nauseous, thinking "uh oh... Must have had more to drink than I thought. " Suddenly I felt so bad; I was sure I was going to be sick. I leaned over, but nothing happened. My stomach seemed fine. That was when I noticed a dark figure had stopped right there between me and the dunes about twenty feet away. It was backlit by the distant lights of houses along Palm Boulevard, but I could not make out even an outline of who was standing there.

It was a little unsettling. Hunched over with one hand on my knee, I pointed at it and said "I see you, shadowy figure, standing over there." There was no reply, just a dark presence kind of watching me. Without taking my eyes off it, I resumed walking and was relieved that the shadow also resumed moving in the opposite direction. As my head began to clear it occurred to me how odd the figure was since the light of the moon to my right should have given me a better view of whoever it was. When I looked back the figure was nowhere to be found. There was just an eerie silence. Starting to feel a little spooked, I took the first path off the beach. It began to dawn on me that the strange feeling of sea sickness had vanished as quickly as the Ghostly Beach Comber.

Submitted by Mambo Johnny, Isle Of Palms, South Carolina
From Ghosts of America 6

. . . .

47.

Mean Man

We lived in Custer Terrace. One night my little boy jumped into bed with me, and I told him "you are too old to be sleeping with me. I have a Parent-Teacher Conference in the morning, and you have to quit waking me up! " I picked up my little boy and carried him back to his room. When I walked in the room was ice cold, and I felt the most evil presence. I had never felt that way before, but when it is present, you know it is just evil! We ran back to my room and jump in the bed! I could not see it, but I could feel it all around me! My little boy was shaking and too scared to cry! I did not know what to do, so I just prayed out loud! My little boy started to scream "shut up mommy you're making it worse. Shut up!" He had never spoken like that to me before! It felt as though it was going right through me, and I was terrified! I could literally feel the separation between my spirit and my body! I started cussing at it, and it went away. I could hear it in the rafters like wood moving!

I thought I might have imagined the whole thing, but after talking to the neighbor, she said she had a similar experience! So I went to visit the chaplain. The priest came to our place and placed holy water over every entrance and window. We did not have any more problems. Four years later we moved to another place on Arrowhead Road. Besides the constant bad dreams I had whenever my husband was not home and the eerie sensations of being watched, the big one came when we were all home. We had been barbecuing in the backyard. I was in the kitchen when my daughter came running in saying "mommy there is a mean man bothering me. " I went outside to check it out, and there was no one there. She came in again, and she went to play in her room. My husband joined me in the kitchen. My dogs' ears stood up, and we heard the back screen door knob turn, the door opened and slammed shut! My husband took off outside trying to find what

126

just went out or came in. We were totally freaked! I later asked my daughter what this mean man looked like. She responded "he had boots and a funny hat."

Submitted by Michelle, Fort Benning, Georgia
From Ghosts of America 2

. . . .

48

The Upstairs Neighbors

Winter Garden, Florida

When my wife, my one-year-old daughter and I moved to Florida we rented an apartment in Winter Garden. The unit had never been rented before. It was a new construction. We rented a first floor unit, and the unit on the second floor on top of us was empty. The stairs for the second floor apartment are side to side to my daughter's room wall. The stairs for the second floor are private; you can only enter through a door on the first floor. Strange things started two or three months after we had moved in. I have always been curious about ghosts and the supernatural because of some experiences before in my life. My first experience in the apartment was a rat-size shadow running side to side. This happened very often. I thought it was my eyes playing on me. I talked to my wife and I started joking about it, telling her that we might have rat spirits running around. Right after I told her we both saw the same rat-size shadow moving on the floor in front of us.

Weeks passed and one day my daughter was in her room laughing, so I went to check on her. My daughter was looking at the roof and laughing. She was only one year old at the time, so I thought it was cute and did not pay much attention to her looking at the roof. My daughter always slept in her crib in her room, and every day she started screaming and crying at around 2 o'clock in the morning. We took a playpen and put it in our room, and she never woke up around that hour in our room. My sister came for a visit with my nephew for the whole summer. She stayed in my daughter's room. I never told her about the experiences in the apartment to see if she experienced something by herself. Well, the summer passed, and she went back to her house. I called her one day, and I asked her if she experienced anything in my apartment. She said "no. " She said the only thing that was annoying her while there was the second floor neighbor. She said

128

that late at night apparently he was running up and down on the stairs that faces my daughter's wall. I was surprised she said that to me because the second floor apartment was empty. When I told her that the apartment was empty she of course freaked out. She also told me that she heard kids playing on the stairs during the day sometimes, but she never heard the door open or close. I was freaked out because I remembered my daughter looking at the roof and laugh.

After that things got a little worse. My daughter's TV turned on by itself two times during the day when I was at home. After that I started to hear someone was running from side to side on the second floor during the day and night, but I thought maybe it was the AC or something like that. The worse feeling I got was in my room months later. I was watching TV, and my daughter was in the living room with my wife. I felt like something or someone small was seated on the corner of the bed and touched my feet. I thought it was my daughter crawling and trying to stand up in the corner of the bed, but when I looked there was nothing. My daughter was with my wife in the living room. Another night I was wakened up and felt like I could not move. I felt as if someone was holding me down on my chest and legs. I started to pray, and I was able to move. After that we decided to move as soon as our contract ended. After we had moved out we never experienced anything paranormal again. I do not know what was wrong with the apartment or the area. These apartments were new when we moved in. I do not know what was there before this building, so I cannot tell. I am glad we just rented and we did not buy that "condo apartment" like we had planned to.

Submitted by CJC, Winter Garden, Florida
From Ghosts of America 3

. . . .

129

49

Still Terrified

New Port Richey, Florida

Before we moved into our house an elderly lady had died in the middle of the room which is now my daughter's room. All that was in there before us moving in was a rocking chair. I believe she died of old age. When we first moved in nothing was happening. It was fine, but her room would always be the coldest in the house. And all this paranormal activity happened one night when my two children (my twelve-year old daughter and eight-year old son) had a sleepover in my daughter's room with a couple neighborhood friends. There were complaints about getting the blanket ripped off of them out of nowhere and unexplainable noises coming from the closet. Then after that one day at 6 o'clock in the morning as we were getting ready to leave to work and I was walking to the door I felt someone walk past me. I knew it was her. I could hear the sound of her knee cap cracking.

A month later around midnight an ambulance came to my house with a stretcher and breathing mask. They said that someone had called from the home phone. We had no home phone, and none of the kids had cell phones. Later on the ghost or whatever started getting threatening to my younger son while everyone in the house was sleeping. He woke my daughter up crying telling her that the doors were opening and closing throughout the house. He said that he felt cold breezes and went into shock and could not move. We did not really believe him until a couple of nights later. That night he woke us up saying that he was choked and was gasping for air. There were red marks around his neck. We stayed and prayed hoping that whatever that was there would leave peacefully. We thought she had left because we were not bothered for two years.

Then one day when it was just my children in the house; both of them heard a growling sound and a deep voice saying "stop

130

making that noise!" Then a month later we were in my daughter's room, we heard a sound and saw that the fence was shaking like crazy. When we ran out, we found that no one was moving the fence. Then the door slammed, and we walked back in the house, and something seemed different. After that incident my son had not been bothered. However, my daughter was. She told me she felt like she was always being watched. She stopped sleeping in her room for a while. Then her stereo would switch the volume randomly. She took a picture in the room. In the background on her computer screen she saw a demon. I was so terrified. We have since left the house. It has been three years now since we left, but we are still terrified.

Submitted by Donald, New Port Richey, Florida
From Ghosts of America 3

. . . .

50.
Not Seen But Felt

Barnesville, Georgia

I had some experiences in a house that belonged to my boyfriend at the time. One morning after he had left for work I was lying in bed. I know that he left for work around 5:30 am. At around 7:00 am I woke up because I heard someone walking up the stairs. Of course I thought that it was my boyfriend. When the footsteps made it to the door, the door opened about three inches. Then when no one entered I got up and checked the entire house. No one was there and all the doors and windows were locked.

The stereo system would turn on by itself. The first time that it happened was shortly after my boyfriend told me that he had a ghost living there. I thought that he was playing a trick on me. I told him to cut it out. He was in the kitchen (the stereo was in the living room.) He told me that he did not have the remote because it was on the hand rail of the stairs. To make thing creepier the stations changed.

The back door would sometimes open and close by itself. Now mind you, this is an old house. The door is very heavy and hard to open. I was sitting on the couch and I knew that I closed the door. I heard the door click and then opened all the way. It then closed back almost all the way. And it did this slowly. I was facing the door. I thought no way that did not just happen. When I was alone in the house was when things would happen.

The only thing that would happen when my boyfriend was there was the stereo turning on. When you were standing in the back yard, if you looked up that the bedroom windows (which was our bedroom) you could see the curtains move back as if someone was looking out. One night when my boyfriend and I were sitting on the couch watching TV, I felt like someone walked into the room and was standing about two feet away from us looking at us.

132

I did not see them, but I could feel them. Now this all happened within three months time.

Submitted by Liz, Barnesville, Georgia
From Ghosts of America 3

. . . .

51

Up For Parole

Fort Walton Beach, Florida

Lewis Turner Boulevard is haunted. My family used to own a flower shop in 1998. When my mother purchased the business the previous owners told her to "watch out for the ghosts; they like to take things". Almost immediately after opening our doors for business the knives used to cut the foam for arrangements started to disappear during the night hours. I was the delivery driver for the business, so I witnessed every possible unexplainable occurrence that ever happened there. A band I used to be in practiced in the large supply warehouse on the property after hours. We owned the business for a few years and witnessed mostly the disappearance of knives and other sharp objects and the rearranging of ribbons and spray paints. We never saw any ghostly images or anything.

One afternoon the guitarist and I were practicing in the adjacent warehouse. We were there for a few hours. The warehouse was equipped with a wall unit AC, which was blowing cold the whole time we were there. After the practice my friend reminded me to go turn off the AC before we left. I walked over to the unit to shut it off, and as I reached over to turn off the power it turned off by itself. I figured it had reached its set temperature and shut off automatically. However, a closer look revealed that it was not plugged in to the wall receptacles at all. We searched for an alternative power source, but there was not one. Needless to say we screamed and ran out of the building. Several months had passed, and all of the same kind of stuff was going on, and my band had fully formed. I was no longer the drummer and had become the singer. The current drummer was a very skeptical person and did not believe in ghosts, spirits, or anything in that matter. He would always sing the "Ghostbusters" theme song and make jokes to the "spirits" saying "come get me!" when he was in the building. One night during practice for an upcoming concert we stopped after one of our songs, and my drummer screamed out "they aren't no ghosts in here!" Almost as soon as he got the last word out of his mouth a large wicker basket used for arrangements flew from across the warehouse and hit him in the head.

Our two guitarists, the bass player, three girls (who were our audience), and I all witnessed this happen. The basket flew horizontally about fifteen feet off of a shelf where no one was standing and hit my drummer in the head. After this happened my girlfriend and I decided to research the property and see if anything had ever happened there. We went to the local daily news and just asked the lady working how we could go about finding out anything about the property. She told us all she needed was the address, and any news in the past 40 years would show up. Sure enough in the 1970s it used to be a feed store for farm animals owned by an elderly couple. The article said that a man had robbed the building. He tied up the couple and then butchered them with an axe before burying them there. The same time my drummer was hit in the head we had a lot more items missing and being rearranged in the shop than usual. Coincidently at this same time a new article my mother had showed me was just published stating that the man who murdered the couple was up for parole.

Submitted by Erik, Fort Walton Beach, Florida
From Ghosts of America 5

. . . .

52

Things In Our House

Metairie, Louisiana

My daughter who is four years old has been seeing things since we moved into this house, along with me and my son and my oldest. My husband works about twelve hours a day, and he does not experience it as much. When he does he always has an explanation of some sort for it all. I on the other hand just feel like there is something more to it. Here are some of the things that have occurred.

Our daughter came in one day panicking about a little boy tied to a chair outside behind the shed in which I checked simply because you never know your neighbors. There was nothing. My daughter talked about the little girl who was burned. My daughter would smell smoke, and tell me it was the little girl. The pictures on the walls have been found upside down in the morning flying off the wall, and all the cabinets and drawers in the kitchen would be open at 6 am. We have all tile floors, and you could hear footsteps. Especially on the tile that the grout was coming undone; it would grind when you stepped on it, and you can tell where the footsteps were going. We have heard heavy breathing and muffled voices.

I have actually thought someone broke into my house. We also heard "hey" in a whispering voice. My son who has always slept with no night light and with his door shut out of nowhere started screaming a while back at night. He said there was a yucky head in his room. (He was two years old at the time it started.) He has now been sleeping with his toy shotgun, a night light, and his door open. He also had conversations at 2:00 - 3:00 am. Sometimes he would be screaming bloody murder at those times which he did not do if he slept in his sister's room.

We have always had a feeling of being watched or someone right next to you. When I was in the shower (at 1:00 am) the bathroom door started rattling. I thought someone was trying to get in to use it. No one was awake when I jumped out to open the door. My in-laws have experienced some of it as well such as a picture flying off the wall but not falling. It came out a good two feet. One time my daughter came to me saying "do you hear them mommy?" I asked her "what?" She said "they are saying our names. Can you hear them?" My oldest daughter (seven years old) told me one morning that she woke up because someone tickled her leg. She said when she looked her dad was squatting on the floor. Then he got up and walked out. The thing was that I actually stayed awake all that night until morning (stressed and could not sleep), and my husband never moved out of bed. This one actually really freaked my husband out.

On another occasion I was sitting at my kitchen table with my back to the wall. It was only me and my four-year-old daughter. I had started getting the feeling that something was not right. Then she pointed behind me and said "um um um" I asked "what?" She responded "there is someone behind you mommy. " I said "no, there is not," and she said "no. Look. Mommy, they are all behind you now. Mommy, get up! Mommy! Mommy, they are behind you. Get up!" I started to look behind me because honestly I believed her. At that moment she covered her eyes and screamed. I jumped up and grabbed her up in my arms and ran out of the room. I did not know what was there, but it scared her and me.

Later one day I was lying in one room, and my kids were in another watching a cartoon. I heard footsteps as if someone was wearing tennis shoes. I got up to check. There was nothing, so I went and sat back down. I heard it again. This time I thought it was one of my kids, but they were all still in the room watching the cartoon. I went back trying to shake the feeling and sat down. I heard it again. Knowing my husband was not home, nor could he get in because we have chain locks on all our doors, I got up again to check. Nothing. I started feeling very creeped out but tried to tell myself it was nothing and sat back down. When I heard it again, my broken tile ground, at the point whatever it was would have been by the doorway of the room I was in. As I got up, my oldest daughter screamed. I ran out, and she said she saw a shadow. She pointed right at the spot where the busted tile was.

It has just been a lot of strange things that have happened. I cannot seem to find a way to find out the history of this house, property, or neighborhood, and this is only some of it.

Submitted by Amber, Metairie, Louisiana
From Ghosts of America 6

. . . .

53.
The Now Bookstore

Florence, Alabama

The story goes that around the turn of the century, a man, a woman, and their little girl lived in this house. The little girl was an only child, so she had to play by herself most of the time. She spent most of her time in her bedroom playing with her dolls and an elaborate dollhouse. On her fifth birthday her father told her that after he came home from work he was going to bring her a special present. Well, when he came home at 5:00 o'clock in the evening, his daughter was sitting by the door waiting for him. She jumped up and grabbed the big box that they placed in her arms. She tore open the lid and a little furry face stared out at her from under an old towel. It was a two-week old puppy. She grabbed the little puppy and hugged him. Her mother and father smiled because she now had the playmate that she had always wanted. She took the puppy into her bedroom and played with him the rest of the evening.

When it was time to go to bed, her mother heard the little girl scream. She ran into the room and found her daughter sitting on the floor holding her hand. She complained that her puppy had nipped her finger. Her mother washed the girl's finger and then put her to bed. A couple of weeks later, the little girl became very sick. Her parents put her to bed and called the doctor. The doctor examined her and said that she had come down with rabies and that there was not much he could do for her. A few days later, the little girl and the puppy died of the same disease.

Many years later, the building became a fraternity house. It underwent extensive renovation before the guys moved in. They even knocked down a wall. Supposedly, whenever you do that or make any serious changes (in the architecture), you run the risk of stirring up the spirits of the house. Well, the story goes that during the homecoming parade, people who marched by noticed a little girl sitting inside a window up near a balcony. They started pointing up toward the second floor of the building, and people standing along the street saw her too. She made several other appearances at the window over the years, but she was usually sighted during homecoming. The building is now the University bookstore, and the ladies who work there claim that the little girl's ghost is still there. They will not talk much about her except to say that they have heard noises late in the evening, and one lady has even seen her.

Submitted by Katie, Florence, Alabama
From Ghosts of America 1

. . . .

54.
An Old Sea Captain
Folly Beach, South Carolina

My husband and I lived in Folly Beach, SC. in 1982 while he was stationed at the navy base in Charleston. One evening, just before dusk we were walking along the beach as we loved to do most evenings. While we were walking side by side and talking along the coast we observed a man walking toward us in the distance.

There were very few people on the beach then, maybe a couple behind us down the beach, and no one was in sight before us except this one man. My husband and I were having a conversation and enjoying the sea breeze. As we walked further down the beach the gentleman continued to walk toward us. Eventually after a while our directions took us closer to him and he nodded his head in recognition of me as we began to pass each other.

I realized when he acknowledged me then that he was a distinguished sort of man, perhaps in his late 50s or early 60s. He had gentle eyes and graying hair which was covered with a black cap. He wore dark clothes, a coat over his shirt and dark pants. He reminded me of an old sea captain. The strange thing that happened to us was when he passed us. It was then I turned to look at him. I guess thinking he was pretty unique. Low and behold he was gone!

There was nowhere he could have gone, out of sight in the couple of seconds it took for me to look back for him. I immediately asked my husband "Randy, where did that man go?" He turned around to look with me, and the man was nowhere in sight. We scanned the stretch of beach along the water and up toward the road area, and he was not there. He could not have had enough time to walk anywhere that we would have not been able to see him. We know we saw a ghost on Folly Beach that night, and I will never forget him. The ghost actually greeted me as we passed each other and then vanished into thin air.

Submitted by Debbie, Folly Beach, South Carolina
From Ghosts of America 1

. . . .

55.

My Grandparents' House

Ruby, South Carolina

My parents were visiting my grandmother about two years ago (my grandmother died last year in early spring). As my parents were preparing to leave they heard what sounded like someone calling out saying "Sarah! Sarah!" All of them heard this voice. My grandmother called back saying "yes". When there was no answer assuming it was my uncle next door my dad went to see what he needed. When my dad went to knock on his door my uncle, his wife, and his three-year old son were all asleep. No one else lived in that area close enough to be heard by any of them. Not only that, none of the people down the street knew my grandmother by her first name.

About three years prior to the above event my parents, my brother, my sister, her husband, and their four kids went to visit my grandmother for Christmas. While we were there my brother-in-law thought he heard someone laughing down the hallway, so he looked over to me and said "who is back there in your grandpa's room?" I told him that there was no one in there. My uncle had been back there but had left thirty minutes prior. After hearing that laughter he got up and walked out of the house.

He refused to return until it was time to tell my grandma goodbye. My grandfather died in January of 2001. Since then no one has slept in his room except for my father. One time when my grandma was sick in the hospital we came to visit her. My father was tired and wanted to take a nap. There was a lot of company in the house, so my grandfather's room was the only place he could rest. My father told us later that he had not felt comfortable and did not sleep at all.

After both of my grandparents died my uncle and his family moved into their house. My grandparents had a door in their

143

hallways that they always kept locked. Even after they passed my uncle kept two chains and two bolts on the door. One night while my uncle and his wife were sleeping the door flew open. After that my uncle put the locks back on and went back to sleep. It happened one more time and after that, my uncle had put a board over it to keep it from happening. We will soon see if it helps or not.

Submitted by Stephanie, Ruby, South Carolina
From Ghosts of America 3

. . . .

56.
What Was It?

Rector, Arkansas

Back in the 1980s we thought it was "cool" to go parking. My boyfriend and I decided to go to Mary's Chapel Cemetery. Everyone who has been there knew there was only one way in and one way out. Arriving just at dusk everything was visible. We circled around and parked between rows on a small gravel road. We were facing the main road, so we would have noticed if anyone else came into the cemetery. As we were talking it had gotten dark. Windows parted the way down, we could hear crickets chirping, a rabbit or two playing, and a hoot owl hooting. We were just enjoying the sounds the nature provided at night. All of a sudden a huge bright single light appeared at the tailgate of the of the truck. We both sat there wondering what this light was going to do next. It was eerily quiet by this time. No sounds from night nature at all.

My boyfriend put his already running truck in drive, and we eased up to the main road with the almost blinding light still behind us going from side to side. As we turned onto the main road to head out of the cemetery he pushed on the gas kind of making us fishtail a little, and the light was making every move we were. When we got up to the county road out of Mary's Chapel Cemetery we stopped and looked out the back glass. By this time there were four of the huge bright lights at the entrance just floating around. Then after what seemed like an eternity flew back into the cemetery. I am nearly fifty now, and that night at Mary's Chapel Cemetery has been etched into my mind. I have never been back and never will. I am kind of a skeptic when it comes to ghosts, but that was a night that still has no explanation. It does make me wonder from time to time just "what was it?"

Submitted by Leah, Rector, Arkansas
From Ghosts of America 4

57

Sweet Aroma

Little Rock, Arkansas

While at the Little Rock Arsenal (Mac Arthur Museum of Military History named after General Douglas Mac Arthur) my friend, my service dog Belle and I arrived early because we wanted to see the museum prior to our tour beginning. My friend and I commented on how beautiful the grand stair case was.

The first room I entered (first floor right front room) had numerous artifacts and an actual military jeep. The room behind it (right rear room) had pocket sliding doors that captured my attention and brought back memories of a dear friend's childhood home in St Petersburg, FL that had pocket doors. I did not feel comfortable and did not enter this room. There was a table in the middle of the room, and the walls had pictures of people from bygone days. I returned to the main hall at the grand stairs. I continued in front of them and entered a room that went the length from the front to the rear porch. I knew I only had time to look at a few items. I stopped at the first enclosed case and admired General Mac Author's personal items. His corn cob pipe especially caught my attention. I so wanted to reach through the plexi-glass and touch it. It held my attention for several minutes. As I continued on there were a few letters that I stopped and read, and admired various pictures of General Mac Author during his time in military service.

The first room we entered on the tour was the room with the jeep, followed by the rooms with the table and pictures (the right rear room on the first floor. There were about ten people in the room with me. I smelled a strong aroma of a soft sweet smell. I proceeded around the room attempting to smell each person's perfume/cologne, but no one had a scent of what I had smelled. I went straight to the rear door of the room and entered the hall way. I asked the tour guide about the smell in the room she asked "what smell?" I went on to say "I smelled a sweet aroma in the room we just left but could not find anyone wearing a similar scent. " The lady to my right in the hall said "I also smelled it. It smelled like cherry tobacco. " Belle jerked in my arms, and I smelled it again standing there in the hallway amongst about fifteen people. I said "There it is again. " The same woman stated "it's back and it's strong. " When we finished our tour and were seated on the bus it struck me and I whispered to my friend "who smokes a pipe?" She said "I don't know" and I said "Mac Arthur. "

After doing research I found the Gen Mac Arthur's favorite pipe tobacco was Harkness F. This blend of tobacco contained Cavendish which provides an aroma that is sweet and smooth.

Submitted by Joanne, Little Rock, Arkansas
From Ghosts of America 4

. . . .

58.
Turning Knob

One night in my mom's house which is off of Mt. Pleasant Road. ,
I was alone and was awoken out of a dead sleep by the sound of
the front door knob moving back and forth very fast and loud. I
immediately jumped out of bed and ran to the front door to make
sure that was the sound I was hearing. Sure enough there was the
front door knob rotating back and forth like someone was trying
to break in.

The thing was, this was Hernando. At the time no one ever had to
worry about a break-in because there was never any crime, at least
on our side of town, so we did not worry about locking doors at
night. The front door was completely unlocked. The knob was not
locked, and the dead bolt was not locked. I was of course
frightened and immediately locked the dead bolt and turned on the
porch and living room light to try and deter this person from
trying to get in.

What was odd was when I did this the knob never skipped a beat.
It kept rotating back and forth. I called the police and went and
hid. The police were there in almost seconds it seemed. Because I
left the room to call the police I was not sure when the knob
stopped rotating, but when they got there the knob had stopped,
and they said no one was on my property or on my street.

The next day I was recounting what happened, and I realized that
on the outside part of my door there was no knob. It was a handle
with lever that you would push with your thumb to open the door
which would not cause the knob to move. The lever would only
move the latch part of the door knob mechanism. If someone was
actually trying to break in they would have with no trouble
because the door was unlocked. I had always felt that there was a

presence in my mom's house, and I truly believe that whatever or whoever that was, was in my living room was moving that knob.

Submitted by Anonymous, Hernando, Mississippi
From Ghosts of America 4

. . . .

59

There Was Nothing There

Vinemont, Alabama

I live in a house almost a hundred years old in Vinemont. We have had several strange things happen here. About two weeks after we moved in around 10 o'clock we heard someone run up the stairs. We were watching TV, and the movie was really intense. We both looked at each other and one of us said "It must be our daughter coming in from her date. " Then we said" but it's early for her, I'll check on her when the movie goes off. " In a few minutes the movie was over, and I ran upstairs and called her name. No one was there. We both heard this. It was pretty loud. My husband did not believe in ghosts and still will not talk about it.

On one occasion, I was drying my hair with my head upside down. I heard someone walk up to me over the noise of the hair dryer. I turned it off and expected it to be my husband. I asked "what did you forget?" No one was there. It was someone with rubber or work boots on I was sure. They walked right up to me and stopped. We know this used to be an old farm house. It was part of a hundred-acre farm.

I have seen fog like figures that hovered and moved from one side of the room to the other. Our cat would sit on our table and stare at the ceiling. She would move her head and meow like she was following something. It would give me the creeps, so I would make her move. She would not go upstairs.

My daughter who lived upstairs at the time always felt like something was up there. She reported things moving from where she would put them at night. She said her jacket would always be lying on the floor the next morning. She knew she laid it on her chair. Things would fall off her shelf for no reason. A toy that was given to her by a friend six years earlier suddenly fell on the floor one day. She picked it up and placed it back on the shelf. It came on and spoke to her saying "that's funny". The battery was corroded, and the toy was not turned on. She threw it away. Shortly after this she moved.

I have been awakened in the middle of the night by voices or old music coming from upstairs. I would lie there too scared to go check it out because I knew there was nothing there.

Submitted by Vicky, Vinemont, Alabama
From Ghosts of America 6

. . . .

60.
A Farmer With Overalls

Dalton, Georgia

I moved with my parents from Kentucky to Dalton, GA back in 1997. We rented a nice house on Beaverdale Road. Upon living there for about a month we started hearing faint whispers on the baby monitors, so my dad unplugged them brushing it off as malfunction. The next encounter was when we came home one night, and my mom saw an older man wearing overalls and a red shirt on our back porch. He was looking at us. However, none of us saw this but her, and it really freaked her out.

Another time was when my mom was at work. I was using the bathroom. When I stood up I saw the old man standing there looking at me. He turned. As he walked away, he just disappeared. It scared me so bad I went and stayed with friends till my parents came home. I have seen the same man as my mom. On another occasion the hair dryer came on by itself. I was telling this to my friends at school when one of the girls said her grand dad was killed in our yard. She said he was a farmer, and all he wore was overalls and flannel shirts. My mom burned candles, and we said a prayer for him. We were never bothered again.

Submitted by Ashley, Dalton, Georgia
From Ghosts of America 6

. . . .

61.

Lucas Bay Light

Conway, South Carolina

I am a Christian gentleman that has lived within a mile of the Lucas Bay Road for all my life, and I want to clarify this matter. I know many dedicated Christian people and other people that live near me in the Lucas Bay community that have seen it and would not be dishonest about it. I also know some who live in this area that have never seen it even though they have searched for it many times. You may never see it, but I can guarantee you that there is definitely a light on Lucas Bay Road (now called Gilbert Road) that has been periodically seen for over a hundred years that is totally unexplainable.

I will be honest and admit that I went down there searching for the light many hundreds of times and never saw it. Therefore, I never believed it was real until back in 1971, when it appeared to me and followed my car for several miles. Since I first saw it thirty-eight years ago back in 1971, I have personally seen the Lucas Bay light three additional times. You may go many times and see nothing, but then you may go and see it the next night. It is totally unpredictable. The weather or the moon does not seem to effect when it is seen. It is true that since major logging went on in that area, it has not been seen as frequent as it used to be. Nevertheless it is still seen at various times. If a person has not seen it, they tend not to believe it like I used to not believe it. If you ever see it, you will never doubt it.

Where to see the light; there is some confusion about where to look for people who search for it today. The name of the original and legendary Lucas Bay Road where the light has been seen for over one hundred years was changed a few years ago. It is now called Gilbert Road, which intersects with Little Lamb Road. There is another dirt road about two miles from the legendary Lucas Bay Road that used to be called the Sand Road. It was incorrectly renamed Lucas Bay Road when the name of Lucas Bay Road was changed to Gilbert Road. The legendary Lucas Bay Road had its name for over one-hundred-fifty years. Nobody in the Lucas Bay community knows why the name of the legendary Lucas Bay Road was incorrectly changed to Gilbert Road a few years ago. The local rumor is that it was done to try to stop people from searching for the Lucas Bay light.

Submitted by Steve, Conway, South Carolina
From Ghosts of America 2

. . . .

62.

Brenda In The Pink Dress

Cohutta, Georgia

I was the aunt that was in the story about the little girl named Brenda in a pink dress. I was visiting my niece and her four kids. My mother was also there. I heard a voice saying "mommy, hey mom. " My mother and I looked at my niece and asked her if she was going to check and see what her oldest daughter wanted. She was the only one asleep in that way, but the voice was much younger sounding to me. I thought it was just me. When my niece opened the door to ask her daughter what she wanted she was sound asleep. We woke her up hollering at her. She rose up and told us to go out. She was not calling for us.

We all heard this small child's voice around the age of five to seven years old. My three-year-old niece continued to play with a girl named Brenda. She has also seen my dead husband whom she loves very much. She talked to him, looked up at the ceiling, and asked who the other man was with my dead husband. I think the unknown man was my dead father that my three-year-old niece had never met. This all took place in Cohutta, GA close to Saint Clairs and Midway Market.

The mobile home is haunted with good spirits so far though! Brenda still plays with my niece daily. They played house-and-dress-up today. My niece fixed them some fried chicken even in her little play kitchen set for supper one night. This story is so true of the little girl named Brenda in a pink dress. I have heard her myself!

Submitted by Aunt Nim, Cohutta, Georgia
From Ghosts of America 6

. . . .

63

Leave It Alone

Pine Mountain, Georgia

Several years ago I moved into a rental home in Pine Mountain, Georgia. I was drawn to the house from the moment I saw it. During the years many unusual things occurred there. Family members reported electrical disturbances and footsteps overhead when nobody was there. Motion detectors would go off when I was not home. The monitoring company would contact me to let me know there was motion in the hallway, but nobody was home, and there were no pets in the house. This happened several times. During the night, I would occasionally hear the sound of windows being locked and unlocked in the kitchen.

On an occasion, a friend of my grown child was unable to open the door of a bedroom in which he was sleeping. He pulled the pins out of the door and still it would not open. The door had no lock on it, so we were mystified. He thought his friends were playing jokes on him and crawled out of a window, walked around to the rear deck and let himself in through the back door. He used the bathroom and noticed his friends were fast asleep. As he walked back to the bedroom he was staying in for the night, something pushed him hard from behind. The door fell into the room with him on top. He was badly shaken and slept on the sofa that night. He left the next morning.

All these years later, he stands by his story. I investigated the house and found there had been a sudden death in the home. It may have been a suicide. Almost immediately after this discovery, I became very sick for several months. Once I moved, the illness subsided and has never returned. There are many other events that occurred in that house. I think the main spirit is benevolent. I do think I stirred up some things better left alone when I started investigating the death that occurred in that house. I was not afraid of the house, but I truly believe there is something there. Pine Mountain is a great place to live, and I miss it to this day.

Submitted by Brenda, Pine Mountain, Georgia
From Ghosts of America 4

. . . .

64.
Brenda And Her Mamaw

Cohutta, Georgia

I moved into our home on Cleveland Hwy in Cohutta about two years ago. Since moving in we have heard a little girl laughing and have seen shadows of a person and a child as well. My three-year-old said her friend Brenda lived in her brother's closet. She said Brenda lived here with us, and this is Brenda's Mamaw's house. I asked what Brenda looked like, she said as tall as my 11-year-old daughter. Brenda has yellow hair, and she wears a pretty pink dress, and her Mamaw is big and has short hair.

Lights would go on and off, and we heard a girl say "Mommy" when it was just my aunt and I here. I did not think and replied "what?" Then my aunt reminded me that we were alone. It gave us cold chills. My husband who is a non believer now says he cannot explain what we hear, but it is something. We still hear toys and dolls going off and see shadows daily. I just pay it no mind.

Submitted by Ashley, Cohutta, Georgia
From Ghosts of America 6

. . . .

65.
Emily

My daughter and her husband lived in a haunted house located in East Montgomery. From the day they moved in strange things began to happen. When they would leave the house, they would turn off all the lights, upon returning every light would be on. All the dresser drawers would be open with clothes strewn everywhere. One day they left to go to a ballgame, and when they returned the washer was turned backwards. However, the most chilling was the child that spoke to them through the computer. Now, bear in mind that it was not online. The computer was simply plugged in, but with no internet access.

One morning my daughter woke up and on the blank screen were the words "mommy where are you? " My daughter was alone in the house, so no one could have done it. After she confided in me, I went over that night, and we decided we would talk with whatever it was. To keep it honest we decided that neither of us would leave the room, so there would be no question of anyone playing a trick. I sat down at the blank screen and typed in "What is your name?" Instantly, an answer appeared; not as if it was typed in, but, it just appeared, "Emily", I said "How old are you". The answer was "5". Then I said, "Emily, were you sick? She answered "yes am sick, typhoid. " At this time my daughter began to cry, and I had a cold chill. We kept going. I said "When did you die?" She replied "1888". Then I said, "do you know me? " She said "No ma'am, do not know you, know Mandy (my daughter). She sick, I help".

At that time, I stopped, not wanting to know anymore. Later we found out that my daughter was sick with thyroid disease. We were both so frightened we left the house. Her husband was out of town, so she stayed with my husband and me until her husband returned. Upon her return, the kitchen floor was littered with old toys, like small cars and a top. Then the toaster came on, but was not plugged in. A few days later a friend came over and brought her little boy, he asked if anyone else was in the house. When Mandy told him no, he asked "well, who just came out of the bathroom dressed in a nightgown? " He described the sighting as a little girl who went into the bedroom. They were so frightened that they went on the patio trying to decide what to do. When they were going back in the house all the doors were bolted shut; the lights in the house came on, and there were sounds coming from the living room even though no one was in there.

Needless to say they decided to move, and did so very quickly. A few weeks later, Mandy's stepdaughter drew a picture. It contained a church, a cross on top with a graveyard behind. Beside a tombstone was a small child, and beside her was written the name "Emily". My daughter's stepdaughter had only stayed in the house for two nights. We did not ask her any questions; she was only five.

Submitted by Linda, Montgomery, Alabama
From Ghosts of America 2

. . . .

66.
Apalachee Heritage

Dacula, Georgia

We purchased a house in Apalachee Heritage in Dacula, Georgia. We moved in at the end of October in 2011. It is a beautiful home and a quiet subdivision. Having moved to Georgia from Iowa I rarely thought about ghosts or history of the land. My other half works from home. I cannot even tell you when things began to get ugly, but I moved out in April of 2013, when he was out of town visiting family, without his knowledge. I felt great terror of him by the time of my escape. A friend of mine took some pictures of our dogs playing together while I was packing and moving. A few days later she sent them to me and told me to look closely at them. Out of about ten pictures, four of them had orbs. One of the orbs was super scary looking. It had swirls throughout. I still get goose bumps when I look at it.

My other half and I met in Iowa, dated, and lived together for about a year and a half prior to moving to Georgia. We rented a house in Buford and lived there for the first year and a half prior to buying and moving into the home we purchased in Dacula. I was so excited. It was everything I thought I would never be able to afford in Iowa. You get so much more home for your money here compared to Iowa! Little did I know this would become a house full of anger, crying, and fighting constantly.

The first thing I remember that seemed out of character for my other half was strange. I remember we had recently moved in, and I was out in the garage smoking. I did not smoke in the house, but it was chilly outside. He had come out to join me and noticed I was wearing my slippers. He jumped on me about wearing them back inside after being in the garage with them on. First of all this was my house too and how dare he speak to me like I was his child and not his partner. Second of all, the garage floor was very clean, and it was not the big deal that he made it out to be. I do not remember if I said anything to him about it but tucked it away in my memories.

Slowly but surely all of that kind of behavior escalated from my partner. I would be crying hysterically in a corner somewhere in the house. It seemed I could not get him to stop until I screamed at him. Before long I was yelling bad things to him about himself as well. One can only endure so much. I would hate myself for yelling. It was not who I was. I hated fighting. There was no reason to ever fight when you are a mature adult and your children do not live with you and have their own lives and family. These are supposed to be the calm and happy years of the empty nesters.

I got to a point that I felt as though I was on pins and needles in my own home. Being that he was working from home, I was rarely home alone. I worked on the weekends outside of the home doing sales. Monday through Thursday I would clean the big house that never seemed to be dust free and take the dogs to the nearby dog park daily. My golden retriever and golden mix became my sanity. I do not know how I would have made it without them. I found myself and my life spinning out of control becoming depressed and suicidal while my partner seemed to turn into a very angry person. Someone I no longer knew. I would take long baths or just lie in bed crying. My golden would always stay by my side and give me a reason to snap out of it. The arguing was a daily thing that would last up to hours of going round and round about the same stuff over and over again.

I was made to feel like my best was not good enough. I was being beat down. My inner soul was fighting to survive. The fun, happy and loving person that I have always been, where did she go? Why had my partner turned into something that felt so evil? The look on his face said it all. Even when friends would come over they could feel it and see it. I sometimes would feel like someone was watching me through the windows at night. The air in the

162

home seemed to become heavy all the time. I would become unnerved and would go around and close all of the wood blinds. One time I was playing ball with my golden retriever, and I threw the ball into the kitchen. Normally he would always run after the ball and bring it back right away. For some reason on this particular night he seemed to be frightened of the kitchen. He did not want to go get the ball. He acted like someone was in there, and he was frightened. I would know if someone had come into the house, so of course this was silly. I coaxed him into going to get the ball. Wanting to please me, he finally darted a few steps into the kitchen and stopped to look around the corner. Then he darted past the island and looked around that corner again before taking the few more steps to grab the ball. He then quickly scurried back to me. This was the oddest behavior I had ever witnessed from him. I decided to get up and look in the kitchen myself and turned on the light. I found nothing.

I was aware that dogs could see spirits, so it affirmed something tucked in the back of my mind that maybe this house has ghosts. I am hearing impaired so I do not hear sounds that would spook most people. I often wandered around the house without my hearing aids in. I had learned to depend on the dogs as my ears by watching them and their body language if needed to be alerted of something or someone. As I stated in the beginning, I now have pictures of the orbs when I moved. They are some kind of confirmation of what was nagging at me all along. Something to say I was not crazy. We both suspected something was wrong in the house. He would have moments where I felt I could reach the person that I used to know, love, and trust.

We did go as far as trying to use sage in the house. I do not think I ever did it right. I did not know who to contact. I did feel like making any step towards admitting to these feelings would somehow label me as crazy. I think there is something very wrong in and evil in that house. There must be something that was the root to all of this senseless anger and fighting. I feel like I let it win when I moved out. I did not know what else to do. Recently I decided to research the history of Dacula and the land. I found out that a man apparently killed his wife, two of their sons, and then took his own life on October 31st, 1910. For some reason this was not talked about and seemed to have been hidden from Dacula records, but I was able to confirm it in neighboring city papers. Some were shocked that the story of the triple homicide and suicide were never talked about, and it seemed to have been covered up from the history of Dacula. That is the furthest date I can confirm of violence in the area so far.

Dacula has some interesting history, and it is sad to say it seems as though these subdivisions could and have been built right over graves. The thought of that seems so sacrilegious and inhuman. I know right before I moved, it was reported that a man shot and killed his wife, called police, and turned himself in. This was a few streets away in the very same development. I now wonder how much this type of things is going on behind closed doors in the area.

Submitted by Holly, Dacula, Georgia
From Ghosts of America 6

. . . .

67

It's the Location.

Long Beach, Mississippi

It's not the house; it's the location. Now, a vacant lot, the southeast corner of Second Street east and Cleveland Avenue in Long Beach has long since borne misery to those who resided in the misshapen, unusually designed stucco house. Perfectly normal families would successively rent the house, and in a matter of weeks or months, the residents would transform into malcontents, nothing made them happy. Troubles dominated each member of each family.

None seemed to be spared. They gradually became darker and darker, more and more unsociable, problematic, delighting in causing neighbors grief and instilling fear and distrust. Most inhabitants would move out of the house under the cloak of darkness, leaving no trace of themselves, no information about their new whereabouts.

After hurricane Katrina destroyed the structure it seems however, the spirits linger still upon the grounds. Even though the property is unkempt, just driving by in a car creeps out any commonly perceptive person. This neighborhood is notorious for "traveling" entities that seem to breeze up and down the block between Nicholson and Cleveland Avenue, on Second Street east only. In the middle of that block, on the north side of the street is a new construction built onto the original front steps of a house destroyed by Katrina.

As legend would have it, priests were imported from nearby Houston, Texas, to perform traditional Latin exorcisms to disrupt the paranormal activity that kept the family that had lived there for twenty-two years on its toes. Particularly in the rear of the residence, the paranormal activity was off the charts! This includes orbs, visions, cold spots, moving inanimate voices, you name it. The lady that owned the place is rebuilding in exactly the same spot on the property! When asked if she feared recurrences, she simply said "yep. Sure do."

Submitted by Mike, Long Beach, Mississippi
From Ghosts of America 1

. . . .

68.
My Parents' Trailer

Ashdown, Arkansas

My parents owned a trailer by Millwood Lake in Ashdown, Arkansas. While my parents lived in the trailer they would wake up to the bed shaking. They experienced this a few times. After my parents moved out my sister moved into the trailer. She slept in the same bedroom that my parents had. The room would get real cold, and she had trouble warming the room. She would see a dark shadow come out of the closet and crawl by the bed on several occasions. A few times she would try to open the door, and someone was pulling the door on the other side, so she could not open the door.

She said she started cursing at it to let her in, and it just let go as she was pulling on it. Her grandson who was only about three at the time came running out of the bedroom. He said he saw a man in there. She would keep bath toys for when her granddaughter stayed with her hanging in the bathtub, and several times the toys would be knocked down into the tub. Once she was lying on the couch asleep, and she heard the kitchen cabinets opening and closing. She woke up and went and shut the cabinets. She fell back to sleep and woke up to something scooting across the kitchen floor. She looked in the kitchen, and a stool was in the middle of the kitchen. She lived there for about two years and experienced other things in this nature.

Submitted by Sandy, Ashdown, Arkansas
From Ghosts of America 6

. . . .

69.
Evil Ghost

Greenville, South Carolina

I used to live in a converted barn just off of Anderson Road. I witnessed many events in that home. Some of them are as follows... One day while sitting in the living room I noticed a very heavy shadow of an old man or woman walk across the opposite wall from where I was, I thought someone was outside on the large porch.

I looked, no one was there or on the street out front.

Another time I came home from work one evening and was in the kitchen making a cup of tea. The only light that I had on was a small night light so the kitchen was fairly dark. As I stood facing the counter I heard someone, a man, clearly say hello. I wear a hearing aid in one ear and am deaf in the other so I am not given to auditory hallucinations. I jumped and turned with my fists up and looked to see no one.

I lived alone and the house was very large I knew no one should be there. After a moment I said I can hear you, but I can't see you, so please don't scare me like that anymore. Nothing else happened that night.

On another occasion I was in my room sleeping when I was awakened by sounds of crashing and banging around somewhere in the house. There was no way I was going to open my door to look as every horror movie starts with someone doing something stupid like that.

I just sat up in bed and waited to see what would happen next. I fell asleep waiting. The next morning nothing was amiss. There is also a room over the kitchen with a private staircase leading up to it. I hated that staircase and kept the door to it closed at all times.

It gave me a bad feeling. Everyone that came over had the same feeling about it. I later found out that the house was originally the barn to a dairy farm. The house is across the street. The original owners were a family named Scott.

There were parents and two children, a boy and a girl. The siblings were playing next to the barn one day in the 1930s when the brother "accidentally" almost chopped his little sisters head off with a scythe used for mowing hay by hand.

She recovered but spent the rest of her life in a state hospital. The young man grew up and married. The father passed away and the mother eventually converted the barn into a home for herself. She was said to be a mean spirited woman who disliked children and spent all of her days picking weeds out of her yard and warning kids to stay off of her lawn.

The son and his wife and children moved into the small house. Mrs. Scott lived in the barn until the day she died. I know the son's wife divorced him for being a drunkard and a wife beater. She left him and the children and moved to New York.

I was friendly with the couple that now occupied the home across the street and was not surprised to learn that no one ever lived in that home for long. I stayed for a year and I loved it but couldn't sleep there.

The house was too active at night so I moved.

Submitted by Karen, Greenville, South Carolina
From Ghosts of America 6

. . . .

70.
The Black Figures

Enterprise, Alabama

I was sixteen at the time when we moved into a house from the 1950s. It was a nice old fashioned two-story home except for the abandoned house across the street from us. My mom told me that they were constructing the house to make it brand new again and sell out to somebody. The day we moved in and settled down in our new home I was in my bedroom at night with my lamp on beside my bed drawing in my notebook until my lamp flickered on and off twice. I thought nothing of it at the time because the house was old and what not, so I continued to draw and scribble till I heard a loud bang like a gun shot from across the street. I rushed to my window and opened the curtains to see what happened, but everything looked fine.

Nobody was inside at that moment, but the lights were on. My parents and my sister were fast asleep, and I was the only one awake. I decided to close the door in my room and turn my light off before it blew out. Once I did that I shut the curtains in my window and put my notebook away and went to bed. Later that night at about 3:35 am I felt like someone was watching me, and I just could not sleep anymore. I felt uncomfortable. I got off my bed and slowly walked down the hallway towards the stairs past my sister's door and my parents'. When I approached the top of the stair case I looked downstairs, and I saw a tiny figure completely covered in black. Before I could go up to it and see what it was, it turned and walked into the kitchen. I followed behind tip toeing. I entered the kitchen and saw it making its way towards the basement door that was locked with chains wrapped around the handle of the knob. It stopped right in front of the door, and I stopped twelve inches away from it. I stared at the back of it in complete fear.

It turned around and faced me placing its finger over its lips telling me to be quiet, and I froze when it smiled with its pitch black eyes that glowed in the dark. Then it walked off into the living room. I made my way into the living room in search of the little shadow, but when I entered it was too late; it was gone. I sighed that it was over, but this was all really happening, so that scared me also. I went back up the stairs quietly trying not to wake my parents or my sister and went into my room and went back to sleep.

It had been a week already living in my new house. Every night I woke up at 3:35 am and saw that little black figure walking around the bottom of the stair case and mostly in the living room. It did not see me anymore because I liked to keep my distance away from it. I had not told my mom or dad about what I had been seeing, and neither had my sister Anasia. Anasia and I saw the little black figure, but she also saw something else I did not see. She saw a six-foot man that was covered in black just like the little one I saw, but this man had glass black eyes with heavy steps. I heard him downstairs every night before I got up.

One night my parents went out to dinner, and Anasia went to a friend's house down the road. Of course, I was home alone with my dog Beanie; he was a Golden Retriever. When everyone left I went into the living room and watched TV for about twenty minutes until I saw the little black figure out of the corner of my eye. Beanie did too, but he did not bark when he saw him. He just stared at him like I always did. It stuck his head in the living room motioning its tiny black hand towards me to follow it, so I did. I got up and followed it through the kitchen to the front door. It opened the door slowly and watched me look outside. The lights across the street were on again except for the shadows pacing by the windows. I looked down at the little figure, and it just smiled at me, so I smiled back without thinking. Beanie came behind me and looked at the figure from between my legs afraid to get near it. I stepped out the door and took a hold of Beanie's leash and made my way across the road towards the house across the street.

When I walked across the lawn all the lights turned off. Beanie and I stopped in our tracks staring at the lifeless house in disbelief. I looked back at my house, and all the lights were on inside and the figure was standing in the door way looking at us from across the street. I turned back around and knocked on the door, but it opened. I let myself inside roaming around the pitch black room that I was currently in. I could hear my heart beat in my ears. Beanie licked my hand, and I pet the top of his head. I walked deeper in the house, and I could hear the old wooden floor creak beneath my feet every time Beanie and I took a step. I stopped because I could feel something in front of me, and I could hear Beanie starting to growl. Something pushed me from behind, and I jerked forward without any control of running into something. When I tripped over a ball I fell to the dusty floor and coughed until Beanie came up to me and whined. I felt around the floor trying to grasp Beanie's leash again, but instead I felt liquid under my finger tips.

A light turned on, and I looked around the rotten living room. I lifted my hand up and saw blood on my hands. I gasped and felt dizzy all of a sudden, so I got up and ran back home. I washed my hands off quickly in my bathroom with the door open. When I turned the faucet off I looked in the mirror and saw Anasia's door open in her room. The tall man was standing in the doorway staring at me, so I shut the door in the bathroom and locked myself inside. I leaned against the door, and I saw the curtain move. I opened the curtain. Nobody was in the tub, but once I did something started to bang on the door really hard. I screamed and leaned against the door again. I woke up the next morning in my bed inside my room sound asleep. I thought I was dreaming.

I got up and went downstairs for breakfast expecting my mom to be in the kitchen already cooking at the stove, but it was silent.

Nobody was awake yet. All the doors were closed in the hallway to Anasias room and my parents. I turned to enter the kitchen, but I heard my mom screaming, and I zoomed upstairs breaking down the door to my parents' room and saw my mom being choked in bed by the tall black man. When he felt my presence he looked over at me smiling, "you're next!" He told me in a deep scratchy voice that filled the whole room with complete coldness. When I ran up to help my mom he disappeared and just vanished into thin air. My mom sat up gasping for air. I looked around the room yelling "show yourself!" It never did.

After that incident with my mom and the black man my mom started to search online for a new home for us to move to. Once Anasia and I told her about the little black figure and how we woke up each night, she started to take Beanie everywhere with us no matter where we went. Things started to calm down a bit after a week. It was an average Saturday afternoon and my mom was busy on her laptop making phone calls for our new home. Anasia went to swimming practice, and my dad was at an important meeting at work. I wanted to take Beanie out for a walk down the street just to explore a bit, so I did. I told my mom that Beanie had to use the bathroom, so she let me go. When I got outside I saw the house across the street. This time there were actually people inside and outside the house fixing. They removed the door and windows with new glass and replaced the old wooden floors with tile and rug.

Submitted by Chelsea, Enterprise, Alabama
From Ghosts of America 7

. . . .

71.
Nun

Statesboro, Georgia

We live on Echo Way. Something categorically dark is in this area. When we bought our home a few years ago, I had an experience with a large dog. Twice it scared me, but it was not 'there'. In my home I have had the TV cabinets opened wide when nobody was around. My son has seen the lady in black (he was very little at the time, and after many questions we were able to determine he was trying to describe a nun.) This 'nun' was pacing around his bed one night and had an upside down crucifix. My daughter, and I have both seen a little boy (about six years old) on the second floor on several different occasions.

I have seen a brunette woman several times. I have heard coughing when nobody was home except me, balls bouncing, door knobs turning, and have had my clothes tugged on many times. I have had 'it' actually run what felt like long bony fingers down me many times at night. What has helped (it has actually been pretty quiet lately) was to walk through each room saying 'Jesus Christ is my Lord and Savior. ' I also wear a bracelet with St. Benedict emblem. My daughter and her friends had a creepy experience in some woods close to our house. It was too long a story, but it freaked me out. There was also a murder-suicide on the next street over just a couple of years ago. This neighborhood used to be a plantation, so there is no telling what sort of history is here.

Submitted by Anonymous, Statesboro, Georgia
From Ghosts of America 7

. . . .

72.
A Point Of Light

I found this website while on my relentless year-long search for an explanation for what my husband and I experienced at the downtown marina in Houma a few years ago. We live in the neighborhood and were out for a walk around 10:00 one night. When we decided to sit on the edge of the dock at the playground under the Twin Span bridges and dangle our feet over the water to watch the tugboats go by. After a few minutes, my husband looked over my shoulder and said "what is that?" I turned to look, and it was a ball of bright about the size of a baseball, moving towards and around us, making a sound that sounded just like a fluttering of wings or old time film strip machines. It went out over the water, and I remember telling my husband to stay away from it. I was afraid that it might not mean us well even though it was beautiful.

I remember having an uneasy feeling and the thoughts flash through my mind of all the horrifying things that I know have happened at this spot (I grew up in the neighborhood and remember many drowning, suicides, police shootouts, and drug activity and related violence --including a scalping happening here). After a couple of minutes it turned into about a six foot tall and wide butterfly made up of luminous green and blue light. I remember being stunned because it was looking straight at me. I mentally wondered if it was trying to communicate with me, and it flapped its left wing at me in response. Then after a moment it disappeared instantly into a point of light.

Here is another weird part of the story that has taken me years and lots of research to figure out. My husband did not see the butterfly. He saw the light, but he said it looked dull like headlights underwater, and he saw it fly away, not disappear into a point of light. After my research the best explanation I could

175

come up with was while I thought the orb turned into the butterfly, what probably happened was that the orb did have mal-intent and perhaps the butterfly was what was called a spirit guide and interceded for me. Maybe that was why I saw it, and my husband did not.

Freaky beyond belief, but I have since watched hundreds of hours of paranormal investigations, read countless stories, and I have seen that light and heard about quite a bit. The clearest video evidence I have found was from Ghost Hunters International, the Trinidad and Tabago episode. They caught a ball of light that looked just like what I saw at the marina flying around a cashew tree where several slaves were hanged many years ago. Also part of the experience, when we got back home, our front door was hanging wide open.

Submitted by Michelle, Houma, Louisiana
From Ghosts of America 7

. . . .

73.
The Creepiness Of The Unseen

We live in a subdivision in Riverview in the Summerfield Area. Our house, not very old, was built in 2004, but we have had a lot of activity. Most of it is in the living room. There are two spots in our house where I have felt strong presences of someone, like they just stand there watching everything, especially at night. I have heard footsteps more than once. I have seen and felt movement around me when there was no one around.

My son, a four-year-old, has mentioned seeing "shadow guys" around the house, most recently was in the living room. He saw a shadow figure with white light coming from his face rise up from the floor and then descend again. One evening he was watching TV in my room, and he said the bed started shaking while he was on it. He was alone in the room. When I am trying to go to sleep at night I can hear noises in the living room, one after another, like someone just messing around with stuff. It stops if I go out there. The good part is that we do not feel threatened at all, just the general creepiness of the unseen, of knowing that we may not be alone in the house.

Submitted by KC, Riverview, Florida
From Ghosts of America 7

. . . .

74.
Not Seen

Greenville, South Carolina

Thankfully, I have not seen anything yet, but I have had some strange things happening to me and my family. The first event was when I was lying in bed, and I had finally dozed off. When I heard a knock on the door. I went to see who it was, and there was no one there at the front door or the back one. That has happened to me a total of three times. It has happened to my husband one time when he was home alone because my son and I were visiting my family. The next event was when I was with my son (who was only two.) Well, we were on the floor playing, and all of a sudden he stopped what he was doing and looked over at our couch with a serious face and said "no! " And my son and I were the only ones there, and no one or nothing was on the couch. This event happened periodically throughout the week.

After I put my son to bed I would think I heard him in his bedroom playing. I would go in there to make him go back to sleep, and he would be dead asleep. The next event that happened was when my husband and I had just woken up. I was going to take a shower, so I turned on the water and was getting ready to get in. I heard someone say my name, so I went in to the bedroom because I thought my husband had called for me. I went in there and said "what do you need?" He said "I did not say anything, " I went back into the bathroom and someone said my name again, and as you can guess my husband did not call for me that time either.

Now the scariest thing yet that has happened, just happened last week. My husband and I were arguing, and I went to get his phone out of the car to put it on charge. Well when I came back in I caught a glimpse of a box fly across the room and hit my husband in the head. My first reaction to do was ask him why he was throwing things. He said "what do you mean why am I

178

throwing things? Why did you throw this box at me and hit me in the head?"

Now I have never believed in these kinds of things, but for some reason all these things are happening. We have only lived here since April. It is now November. The first event happened about a week after we moved in, and they have not stopped. I live in Conestee, South Carolina.

Submitted by Brandi, Greenville, South Carolina
From Ghosts of America 1

. . . .

75.
Ghost Lights

I married a man from Saucier, MS and moved to this small quiet community. I did not know at the time that I moved in here that we lived right in the middle of where three Indian burial mounds were located. It seemed immediately after I moved into my husband's home that odd things began to happen. I started to get sick. It seemed to start from the very first day that I stepped into the home for the first time. I was able to work for a few more years after moving in, but my health grew progressively worse until I finally had to retire from my nursing career (which I loved) and go on disability.

I should have known from all the things that were happening up to that point that something was very wrong, but I just stubbornly went about the business of trying to live and be a wife, mother, and grandmother. Strange things had been happening all around the house. At times something would also seem to follow me to my mom's when I would go spend the night with her. Strange things would also happen there.

Back at my house things would not be where I would leave them (pardon the pun.) Things would go bump in the night. Small balls of light would appear in our living room, and they seemed to go through the walls into one of our bedrooms. They just floated around in there, or that was what they seemed to do on the first occasion that I saw them. My father-in-law told me that the lights I was seeing were called "the ghosts lights. " He said that if you saw them, someone you know was going to die shortly thereafter. Sure enough it happened that my sweet uncle was diagnosed with cancer and died ten days afterward. He never even exhibited signs of having cancer, nor was he sick or in pain until after being diagnosed.

Not too long after that incident a sweet dear friend spent the night with us, and she woke me up "screaming" to the top of her voice for me to get in there quick. She said she needed help quick! When I opened the bedroom door I saw what seemed to be hundreds of those little lights and one big one. I told my friend what my father-in-law had told me about them, and she was upset to say the least. Anyway the next night she went to church with us as we were going there to play and sing for them. There she received a call from her mother that her uncle was found dead. The poor man had been murdered. Someone had "drowned" the poor guy. If I did not believe before that, I was surely a believer then.

I also unfortunately saw the ghost light one more time that same year, and my husband's aunt died two days later. Needless to say, I never want to run up on that light anymore. Things happened there seemed in clumps or whatever you may call it. It came and went as it felt like it, I guess. Sometimes at night I could hear three or four people talking to one another. At times I really thought that they were talking about my husband, myself, or even my animals as I have specifically heard them call out one of my little dog's name "Schotzy. "

And, yes my little dogs have at times been scared to be out of my sight in the house. I have seen some of the ugliest creatures (for lack of a better word to call them) that you could even imagine walk right through our living room and out through the front wall. It was just like the front wall was not even there. I have heard some of the most terrifying growls or groaning coming seemingly from open air at no particular time (it did not matter whether it was day or night.)

There is one particular room in our house that no one would ever want to sleep in there unless they really "have to" as they put it. As the mattress would sometimes "shake off" the bed frame while they were still trying to sleep on it! No, we do not get a lot of company anymore that wants to sleep over. There is so much more that goes on here, but I am getting tired. I try to sleep now whenever I can (by god's grace.)

Submitted by Roxanne, Saucier, Mississippi
From Ghosts of America 7

. . . .

76.
Never Ending Hallway

Gulf Shores, Alabama

Two years ago, my family and I were visiting Gulf Shores for two weeks. While we were there we made the decision to go to Fort Morgan (which is a brilliant place.) While we were there the area had a kind of eerie feeling to it. I had chills most of the time we were there. The last area we visited was a long hall to the right of the entrance. This hall already has a creep factor as it is only wide enough for one person at a time, covered in graffiti, and seems never ending. The hall seems to go on for what seems like forever. If you do not have a flashlight, do not even plan on trying to go in. The hall has a good bit of turns and gets darker with each turn.

My cousin and I decided to try and see what was at the end of the hall. Being this was our first trip, we had failed to equip ourselves with flashlights. We decided to try and use a phone flashlight and attempt to endure the creepy hall. As we got around the first turn, I began getting chills and almost every hair on my neck and arms stood up, but we carried on anyways. As we got around the third turn, our makeshift flashlight did little to illuminate the impending darkness of the tunnel, both physical and metaphorical.

Now, I am not a claustrophobic person, but I have never felt more suffocated in a small place than in that hall. I had to immediately leave due to the fact that it felt as though multiple beings were pressed against me. I did not want to jump to conclusions and check this off as ghosts, but I can find no other reason as to why I experienced this feeling. I am 100% positive that something is residing in that hallway, and it certainly is not looking to make you feel welcome.

Submitted by Taylor, Gulf Shores, Alabama
From Ghosts of America 6

77

A Quarter Cup of Water

Myrtle Beach, South Carolina

We stayed at a hotel in Myrtle Beach this past summer. When we arrived I looked in the cabinets and fridge to see what I needed to buy at the store. There was nothing in the fridge. We got settled, and it was raining, so we went to visit a friend and to the store. When we got back, while putting the groceries away, there was a plastic hotel cup 1/4 the way full of water in there. I asked my husband if he did it. He said no. Nothing was thought about it; I just dumped the water and threw the cup away. Then we went for a walk on the beach. When we got back, I was getting a drink out of the fridge. On the other side of the fridge there was another 1/4 cup plastic cup of water. I asked my husband again. He said no; he did not do it. I dumped the water once again and threw the cup away. We ate and stayed in the rest of the night. The next morning, while he was in the shower, I went to get the milk out of the fridge. On the bottom shelf there was a 1/4 cup of water. I had chills this time and went and got him out of the bathroom. We both stood there looking at each other with our mouths open. He said now this time I did see you throw the cup away. That was the last of the water scene from the trip.

There was a big Shrines Parade going on that day, so we went to the parking garage to watch. For almost an hour I kept feeling something tap my side. There was no one close to me, and I was standing next to a pillar. Once I finally said something to my husband about it. It did not happen again. On the morning we left and arrived home that evening. My husband was taking his arthritis medicine and asked me what these pills were doing in his bottle. I looked and they were a couple of infection pills that I had left over, that I carry with me while away from home. They were in a prescription bottle of mine that I never touched. How they got in his bottle I do not know.

The room that we stayed in had a for sale sticker on the fridge. I emailed the owner once and asked if there were any reportings of strange things going on there. She never emailed me back. She had a guest sign book, and I left a message that if anyone had a strange experience with the fridge please email me. Once again no emails. I do know that the maids acted as if they did not want to stay in the room. They would throw us our towels and leave; they never made the bed or did anything to the room except the last night. All the other rooms we stayed in, they have always cleaned. We have been staying in this hotel for the several years now, just never this room. I do know that last year while leaving one evening for dinner, in the dumpster we saw a mattress that seemed to be covered in blood. I do not know if this had a connection, but it was a strange experience.

Submitted by Kim, Myrtle Beach, South Carolina
From Ghosts of America 1

. . . .

78

The Ghost Room

Augusta, Georgia

I cannot disclose the name and place of the actual nursing home where I worked as a nurse for a short time before quitting. Shortly after starting I was told by staff that the room immediately past the fire doors on the right was left empty. As the story goes one of the rooms previous occupants after dying had refused to vacate the room. Furthermore, anytime a patient had been put in that room the patient would witness poltergeist activity. The room was permanently kept empty per administration. That was not all, however.

Only at night the front door had a proximity alarm that would sound as a precaution to prevent elderly confused patients from wandering off. All night long the spirit would loudly and violently beat and shake the nursing home's glass double doors that were locked every hour until around 6 am. Then it would cease until late the next night again. One night I was called to a room where a patient was in crisis; she was passing away. Not on my shift I swore.

We began to nurse. Scientifically speaking there should have been improvement even if it had only been prophylactic. However, after all our interventions we all were filled with fear. All of us being trained came to realize the same thing. Something other worldly was choking this patient to death. We all agreed the patient was being suffocated to death. This may seem farfetched, but if you had been there, you would not be so doubtful.

Several reassessments concluded that her airway was unobstructed. Oxygen had been administered along with other ordered interventions. There should have been some improvement, and the decline should have been slowed at the very least. This should not be happening, not like this. That was impossible. Superstition and being Catholic I actually began praying over the patient at the bedside, and so did all staff present. We all began asking our lord to intervene on the patient's behalf if indeed it was actually a spiritual attack taking place. I left the room to make that ill-fated call to the family. Surprisingly one of my staff members ran up and said "she's fine. " "What?" I replied. "She's okay," she continued, "the very same moment you left the room, the woman's oxygen saturation returned to normal, and she came to. " She went on. The woman was down the hall singing old Christian hymns thanking Jesus at that very moment. The songs were from her childhood; she would later tell me.

They sounded like they were from the old time south. This was all very creepy. Fifteen minutes later the other nurse working the opposite wing had a similar emergency with a patient. Apparently she said that a patient was standing talking to her at the nurse' station when at the same moment my patient had come out of her emergency her patient had fallen over. The other nurse's patient had to be sent to the hospital. I was told by the other nurse my prayers had moved the spirit to spare my patient, but had inadvertently led it to do the same thing to one of her patients.

The next night the other staff was gathered on break outside the ghost room. I heard them say that they believed it was the evil ghost from the haunted room. Eager to discuss the previous night' strange event, I hurried down the hall to the other staff. What happened next scared all the staff so much that they would not approach me or hang out with me again. We were standing in front of the ghost room's door, with my back turned to the door.

They all looked and then I turned to see the door knob turn slowly, and then the door opened. The weeks following the doors where I would start to treat my other patients would open for me. It was helping me with my job. Also the call light in empty rooms began to go off again and again. I reasoned this spirit was dangerous. Scared I quit shortly thereafter. However, any nurse will tell you similar stories as these.

Submitted by Bogota40, Augusta, Georgia
From Ghosts of America 7

. . . .

79.
I am Gifted.

Hornbeck, Louisiana

I have had many ghost experiences. I have seen the ghost of a middle-aged woman. Her hair is in a bun; she wears an old middle-aged dress. I have seen her at night walk into my grandparents' bedroom and then disappear. Another ghost I have seen is that of two full-grown black Labrador Retrievers (seen them walking around in my pasture and then disappear). I have heard many strange noises and sounds that have led me to believe that they were indeed made by ghosts. Sometimes I hear howling next to me, but nothing was there. I also hear a female child screaming for help from my closet in my bedroom. Other times I can hear someone calling my name when I am nowhere around anyone. Other sounds that I have experiences include loud barking noises next to me, dog breathing, panting noises next to my ear as I lay on my bed, scratching noises on the screen of my bedroom window, banging noises on the wall in the bathroom, footsteps, computer keyboard typing noises, and whispers.

I have experienced ghosts when I went up to my granny's mama's old house. There I had the front door slam in my face when it was not even a windy day at all, and ghosts in that house have trapped me there for a while. There were many places in the house that I could have gotten out, but somehow it was like they would not let me get out. It only lasted for a short while and when my brother came back up to the house with me, it all stopped, and I was free to get out of the house.

When I was really young, my favorite cat, Sylvester died mysteriously. When I found out, I was devastated so I ran outside and walked up to a fence at the side of our house. I laid my head face down on top of the fence and started crying. Suddenly, I began to hear cat's noises right at my feet, so I raised my head up off the fence and peered down at my feet. There was nothing there, but I could still hear the cat's noises clearly. Constantly, every single day and night, every second, I feel as though I am being watched by something or someone, and it never stops. I have almost gone completely insane because of all this. People say that I have a gift to see unbelievable things. I believe them, and for whoever does not believe, I can promise you that someday you will experience these things, and it will change your life forever!

Submitted by Trish, Hornbeck, Louisiana
From Ghosts of America 1

. . . .

80.

A Man In A Black Cloak

Loganville, Georgia

This happened in Loganville. At the time this happened I did try to contact a local ghost investigation group, but I never received a response. I did eventually get in touch with a ghost investigator that was featured on a TV show, but she did little to quell my nerves. It has been several years since this happened, and though time has dulled the terror somewhat, I am still afraid and unsure exactly what I encountered that evening.

I can't remember what time it was, but everyone in the house was asleep. I'd just turned off the TV and closed my eyes to go to sleep. I heard pots and pans clicking together in the kitchen and thought "great, the cat's in the cabinet again. " I looked toward my bedroom door and saw something on the ceiling. It was outside of my bedroom doorway; its head on the doorway trim - facing me. The face had no features, just a black featureless oval. It looked almost like a fencing mask. The clothing appeared in tattered strips and undulated - as fabric moves underwater. As I studied it, I remember I could just barely make out what looked like a bony heel and lower leg on the ceiling.

You could imagine my complete and utter horror, terror, and fear. All of these were running through my mind. However, the face didn't move; it stayed perfectly still. I started to think it was an optical illusion, that something from the living room (which was on the other side of my bedroom wall) was casting a shadow and creating the illusion that I was seeing. One of my daughters, who was sleeping in the living room that night, walked past my bedroom to the bathroom at the end of the hall. I called out to her, (I'd pretty much convinced myself that the figure on the ceiling outside my doorway was an illusion) and told her, "Alyssa, I think your cat is in the pots and pans again. " Alyssa came to my doorway, rubbing her eyes, and asked "what mommy?" I didn't intend her to come to my door way, I'd only half convinced myself that the figure was an illusion. Now my daughter was standing directly under it. I was terrified! I told her "never mind. " She then proceeded on to the bathroom.

I waited anxiously for the bathroom light to flood the hallway and either expose what this "thing" was or reveal that it was all an illusion. When Alyssa hit the switch the hallway was lit up, and nothing was there. I started to feel stupid, what an idiot I was! After Alyssa was done, and the light was turned off I watched to see if I could discover what caused the optical illusion. And to my amazement, I saw the upper corner of the doorway was illuminated from the kitchen stove light (that I had left on that night.) That light so illuminated the doorway that it was obvious that the figure had indeed been on the ceiling and blocked (more like absorbed) the light.

I went pretty hysterical. I jumped out of bed, woke my husband, and ran to the living room. I checked on my kids, and they were all sleeping on the living room floor that night (a little slumber party.) They were okay, and I asked my oldest, Amelia, if everything was okay. (I didn't want to scare them, so I didn't mention what I saw.) She said yes, and after a thorough check of the house I went back to bed, but I didn't sleep at all.

The next morning I asked Amelia if she'd heard anything, or if anything unusual happened that night. She told me "I didn't want to scare you, but I saw a man in a black cloak standing outside your doorway last night. " We've lived in haunted houses before, and in fact had recently moved from an extremely haunted house in Pennsylvania (our family has long felt that we attract spirits for some reason.) What I saw that night in Loganville was something completely different, and something I hope to never see again.

Submitted by Diana, Loganville, Georgia
From Ghosts of America 7

6496100R00107

Printed in Great Britain
by Amazon.co.uk, Ltd.,
Marston Gate.